Malice

PHRONESIS

A series from Verso edited by
Ernesto Laclau and Chantal Mouffe

Since 1989, when the first Phronesis book was published, many events of fundamental importance to the series have taken place. Some of them initially brought the hope that great possibilities were opening up for the extension and deepening of democracy, one of the main points of focus in our reflections. Disenchantment, however, came quickly and what we witnessed instead was the reinforcement and generalization of the neoliberal hegemony. Today, the left-wing project is in an even deeper crisis than it was ten years ago. An increasing number of social-democratic parties, under the pretence of 'modernizing' themselves, are discarding their Left identity. According to the advocates of the 'third way', and with the advent of globalization, the time has come to abandon the old dogmas of Left and Right and promote a new entrepreneurial spirit at all levels of society.

Phronesis's objective is to establish a dialogue among all those who assert the need to redefine the Left/Right distinction – which constitutes the crucial dynamic of modern democracy – instead of relinquishing it. Our original concern, which was to bring together left-wing politics and the theoretical developments around the critique of essentialism, is more pertinent than ever. Indeed, we still believe that the most important trends in contemporary theory – deconstruction, psychoanalysis, the philosophy of language as initiated by the later Wittgenstein and post-Heideggerian hermeneutics – are the necessary conditions for understanding the widening of social struggles characteristic of the present stage of democratic politics, and for formulating a new vision for the Left in terms of radical and plural democracy.

Malice

FRANÇOIS FLAHAULT

Translated by Liz Heron

VERSO

London • New York

This book is supported by the French Ministry for
Foreign Affairs as part of the Burgess Programme,
headed for the French Embassy in London by the Institut
Français du Royaume Uni

Liberté • Égalité • Fraternité
RÉPUBLIQUE FRANÇAISE

This edition first published by Verso 2003
© Verso 2003
Translation © Liz Heron 2003
First published as *La méchanceté*
© Descartes & Cie 1998

1 3 5 7 9 10 8 6 4 2

Verso
UK: 6 Meard Street, London W1F 0EG
USA: 180 Varick Street, New York, NY 10014–4606
www.versobooks.com

Verso is the imprint of New Left Books

ISBN 1–85984–691–2
ISBN 1–85984–481–2 (pbk)

British Library Cataloguing in Publication Data
A catalogue record for this book is available from the British Library

Library of Congress Cataloging-in-Publication Data
A catalog record for this book is available from the Library of Congress

Typeset in 10 on 12 ITC New Baskerville by
SetSystems Ltd, Saffron Walden, Essex
Printed by R.R. Donnelley & Sons, USA

Contents

Preface

Despite the fact that topics like 'violence' and 'evil' are discussed everywhere today, very little progress has been made in understanding them. One could even argue that most approaches tend to obscure rather than clarify those phenomena. Informed as they are by a rationalist liberal framework according to which the triumphant march of rationality is bound to liberate us from those supposedly 'archaic' remnants from 'pre-modern' conditions, it is not suprising that most studies are incapable of coming to terms with the ambivalent nature of human sociability. The idealized view inherited from the *philosophes* of the Enlightenment explains the incapacity of democratic political theory to grasp the nature of 'the political' and to acknowledge the ineradicability of antagonism.

In recent decades, those shortcomings have become even more evident. Current discourses about the 'end of the adversarial model of politics' claim that we are now living in a 'second modernity' where all issues can now be resolved 'at the centre', through rational dialogue or with the help of impartial tribunals. We are being urged to abandon the traditional categories of 'right' and 'left', and start thinking instead in terms of 'right' and 'wrong'. Since September 11 this narrative has been given a different twist with the affirmation that the new lines of conflict are those opposing rationalist humanism to diverse forms of fundamentalism.

Today, morality has become the master-narrative, replacing discredited political and social discourses in providing the guidelines for collective action. Such a transformation is generally presented as an advance in rationality, and as opening up a new stage in the progress of democracy. This celebration of a consensual approach to politics, however, is not shared by Phronesis, and it has already been challenged by several authors in this series. Indeed, one of our objectives is to contribute to redefining the left/right distinction which, in our view, constitutes an important part of the dynamics of democratic politics. This, as several of our contributors have already argued, entails elaborating an alternative to the rationalist perspective which forecloses an adequate undestanding of the political.

François Flahault's book is a very welcome addition to our enterprise because, in a very original way, it addresses several issues which are at the core of our project. By combining several disciplines – philosophy, anthropology and literary criticism, as well as psychoanalysis – Flahault scrutinizes the origin of malevolence and reveals that, contrary to the view presented by moral philosophy, it is within us that the roots of wickedness are to be found. Through a meticulous and novel analysis of works of literature like Mary Shelley's *Frankenstein*, John Milton's *Paradise Lost* and William Godwin's *Caleb Williams*, among many others, he examines the psychic framework which makes possible the emergence of malevolent conduct. He shows how the forces of life and the forces of malice feed upon the same sources, and that it is a mistake to believe that they can be separated. Taking issue with the widely accepted view that monotheism constitutes moral progress, he argues that by instigating a dualism between good and evil, monotheism has in fact foreclosed the possibility of acknowledging the ambivalence of our fascination with the limitless and infinity. This closure was later reinforced by the Enlightenment, with its idea of the natural goodness of man. Hence our belief in the possibility of a reconciled society where harmony would reign.

This optimistic view, which attributes to human beings the power to form harmonious relationships whatever their differences, has led to what Flahault calls the 'puritanism of good feeling'. By exempting man from the inner source of wickedness, which is transferred on to the external world, the Enlightenment represented a further step in the process – initiated by monotheism – of trivializing the infinite. The purified conception of the self expressed by the rational subject represents an extension – under a new guise – of the idea that, since man was created in God's image, he can only be good. The moral subject of the Enlightenment goes further still, because it manages to eliminate the tension between two extremes which is constitutive of the construction of the self: limitlessness, and the need for other people. Flahault shows how it is only in the register of narrative that the possibility of expressing this tension can still be found. He convincingly illustrates this thesis with the example of *Frankenstein* which, in his reading, dramatizes the desire to be oneself fully and unconditionally.

One of the most interesting aspects of *Malice* is that it provides us with a powerful critique of the political anthropology of the Enlightenment, a critique which has important implications for democratic politics. It has been one of the key ideas of Phronesis that – contrary to Habermas's claim – the rationalism of the Enlightenment did not represent the only possible framework for conceiving democratic politics. We have argued that the opposite was in fact true, and that unless we relinquish the rationalist problematic, we are incapable of envisaging the widening of the field of social struggles characteristic of the present stage of demo-cratic politics. It is our contention that, far from being the necessary basis for democracy, the rationalist view of human nature, with its denial of the negative aspect of human sociability, constitutes its weakest point, since it blinds democratic theory to the nature of 'the political' in its dimension of hostility and antagonism. Hence the importance of acknowledging the tensions set in motion by social exchange, and the impossibility of achieving perfect harmony.

Flahault makes a similar point when he argues for the need to relinquish the search for a genuine solution to the tensions inher-ent in living in society. He insists that it is possible to manage those tensions only by means of compromise, and warns us against the dream of achieving a final solution. Although he is not directly concerned with democratic politics, it is clear that everything he says about the different ways in which the conflict between the desire for completeness and the fact of dependency on others can be managed is relevant to thinking about a democratic mode of coexistence. It is only when we recognize the ambivalence of our fount of limitlessness, instead of rejecting all evil outside us, that a positive relation can be established between the two forces.

This book is full of interesting insights, but one of them is of particular relevance to grasping why a moralistic type of discourse has become so pervasive nowadays. Analysing the consequences of 'the puritanism of the good feeling', Flahault brings to our attention the role played by the mechanism of self-idealization in the constitution of the moral subject. Examining the 'triangle of moral relations' which exists between the villain, the innocent victim and the spectator, he indicates how, by being horrified by the behaviour of the villain and responding with compassion to the victim's distress, the spectator identifies with the victim, thereby idealizing himself. Pretending to have nothing in common with the villain, he succeeds in ridding himself of his bad feelings while keeping their energy which, since it has been converted into indignation, has become legitimate. This seems to me an extremely promising way to tackle the growing appeal exerted by moralism in our societies which have become incapable of thinking in a political way. The consequences of the prevalent end-of-politics *Zeitgeist* is that moral condemnation has replaced political analysis. Instead of acknowledging their internal problems and their own limitations, democratic societies are increasingly looking for 'villains' to demonize, thereby giving themselves a good conscience. This is a very dangerous development which must be resisted before the struggle against the presumed 'forces of evil' has emptied democratic institutions of their meaning. By showing us the mechanisms at work in the so-called 'moralization' of politics, *Malice* adds an important dimension to the political reflection undertaken by Phronesis.

Chantal Mouffe

Introduction

One of the survivors of Auschwitz, Primo Levi, often went into secondary schools to speak about his personal experience. In the early 1980s, he acknowledged his unease when he was faced with the questions pupils would ask. 'What I would like to ask you now is this: would you be able to answer this question: Why are wars fought? Why do people torture their enemies, as the Romans did and as the Nazis have done? . . . Well, I for one don't know how to account for the fact that man is evil and not good, except with vague generalizations. How is one to reply to this question which I am so often asked about human goodness or wickedness?'[1]

Primo Levi was probably better equipped to respond to clever questions than to answer this naive one. The clever questions boil down to something along these lines:

What are the historical, social, ideological, organizational and other conditions which can trigger the logic of destruction and set it in motion?

Ever since the end of the Second World War, this question has been asked a great deal. It is the province of the human sciences, and it is historians in particular who have studied it, seeking to understand how the Nazis could have gone so far as to exterminate millions of human beings who were in no way engaged in warfare. However, when we consider these events, along with the massacres which have taken place in Rwanda, those being carried out in Algeria, or even at a more banal level, whenever we are struck by the violence of economic relations, we do not only ask ourselves questions that are 'clever'. We also react like the pupils Primo Levi talks about, because these singular events cast a troubled light on our conception of human beings in general. Thus, behind the question answerable by the human sciences, in the background there still lurks a 'naive' inquiry which is, in fact, a philosophical inquiry. We could formulate it in these terms:

What are the inner springs of human malice?

This is the question which this book takes as its subject, a question which it is necessary to ask at the present time.[2] Indeed, the temptation to avoid it – in other words, what comes down to the old temptation of self-idealization – does not just lead to all kinds of individual bad habits, but equally supports belief in illusions widely shared. These illusions, as has often been said, are catastrophic whenever they guide the political ideal of entire societies.[3] But they are also dangerous when they collapse, since it is then that the well-meaning, who had learned to associate the desire for good with idealization, either lose the impulse which animated them or else, in order not to lose it, preserve within themselves an idealization which they only pretend to renounce.

The forms of contemporary thought – at any rate, those which are marked by the spirit of the Enlightenment and the progressive humanism of the last two centuries – tend to avoid the question of the inner springs of malice. We can see one example of this propensity in what has been recently published about the crimes of Communism – or, rather, in the lessons which readers often believe they should draw from such studies. In countries which are very different from one another, but had in common the experience of being under a Communist regime, the sum total of crimes committed is overwhelming; without a doubt, Leninist ideology turns out to have been as catastrophic as Hitler's. Taken by itself, this linking of ideas is not false; but it becomes so when it inclines to the belief that it is bad values alone which are at the origin of the evils humans inflict on one another; and that, in the absence of these pernicious ideologies, humanity would avoid wickedness. Indeed, it is not just bad principles that lead people to harm one another; other factors (such as the violence of relations of economic dominance, political disorganization, widespread incompetence and irresponsibility) are just as likely to have this consequence. Moreover, we have no proof that solely *external* factors are involved, and that there is no factor *within* human beings which needs to be taken into consideration. Not only do we have no proof of this, but crimes and massacres, as well as the innumerable manifestations of ordinary malice which run through everyday life and the history of all human societies, impel us strongly to contemplate the opposite hypothesis – that is to say, to ask ourselves the question which the secondary-school students put to Primo Levi.

Why, then, does scholarly and enlightened thought tend to avoid a question which everyone nonetheless asks themselves? The human inclination to self-idealization is not all there is to it; this question has a specific history. The question of the inner springs of malice has been explored within a whole current of European thought ever since Saint Augustine, and this happens to be the current *against which* Enlightenment thought (which is still ours to a great extent) struggled and imposed itself. The Augustinian current conceived of human wickedness within the context of the Christian doctrine of Fall and Salvation, emphasizing the absence of a state of grace because of original sin. This pessimistic idea of human nature connects with a theology of divine grace (man being too corrupted to save himself by his own efforts), and with a justification of the authority and coercion exerted by the political order. Evil becomes heightened – left to themselves, men will go to the bad – in order to make its remedy all the more necessary; thus catastrophe prepares the way for the Sovereign Good (René Girard thinks in a similar way: human desire, a mimetic desire doomed to the deadlocks of rivalry, leads fatally to boundless violence – unless sacrifice or, better still, Christianity . . .)

The more the humanist, rationalist, liberal and emancipatory current developed, the more Augustinian ideas came to seem contrary to the spirit of progress. They even looked downright reprehensible when, helped by Darwin, conservative writers (Carl Schmitt, for example) deployed arguments about the natural violence of human relationships in order to extol the use of force and domination. Certainly, Freud and Lacan, whose view of human nature follows the Augustinian current, are exempt from this suspicion. But psychoanalysis is not a philosophy. It is bound up with the clinical experience on the basis of which it was elaborated, and could not in itself provide an overall conception of man and society.

Hence the situation we are in today: humanist liberal thought, now dominant, dodges the question of an inner spring of malice – both because it no longer wants to hear about the old answer and because, since it now believes that wickedness is caused by external and circumstantial factors, it is not in a position to supply any new answer itself.

To help us understand this situation more clearly, let us return briefly to the period which was decisive in the shift from an Augustinian conception of humanity to a more optimistic one – in other words (obviously with considerable simplification) to the turn of the seventeenth and eighteenth centuries. I shall confine myself to two fundamental reference points.

First of all, a comparison between Hobbes and Locke, and the idea formed by each of these two philosophers concerning man in the state of nature. Hobbes published his great treatise of political philosophy, *Leviathan*, in 1651. He did not seek out man in the state of nature within some hypothetical reconstruction of his primitive state, but found this in what struck him as the 'natural' behaviour of the people around him. And what he saw was a being fallen through original sin: because of the boundless value he sets on himself, each man opposes all others with a violence without end; the result being that wherever justice prevails, it is not through nature, but through reason and coercion. Some forty years later, in 1690, Locke published his treatise *Civil Government*. Here, man in the state of nature is not devoid of self-love, but he is no longer held back by coercion and rational calculation alone. Indeed, for Locke, just reason is also the natural law, and this directs human beings towards equality and sociability. Like other Protestant intellectuals of his day, Locke took on the old humanist heritage of the ancient world's philosophy (notably in Cicero's formulation), substantially diminishing the significance of original sin. Locke therefore moves away from the Augustinianism which, combined with patriarchal and theocratic notions, justified political absolutism.

Nevertheless, as my second reference will show, Locke does not, for all that, repudiate the idea that wickedness has a source within the soul. In this he is like the poet Milton, who, several decades before him, was a militant humanist and advocate for political freedom, while remaining a convinced Augustinian in his exploration of the inner recesses of the soul. Three years after his treatise *Civil Government*, Locke published *Some Thoughts Concerning Education*. This is what he wrote about children's love of dominion:

> I told you before, that Children love *Liberty*; and therefore they should be brought to do things that are fit for them, without feeling any restraint laid upon them. I now tell you, they love something more; and that is *Dominion*: And this is the first Original of most vicious Habits, that are ordinary and natural. This Love of *Power* and Dominion shews it self very early . . . We see Children (as soon almost as they are born, I am sure long before they can speak) cry, grow peevish, sullen, and out of humour, for nothing but to have their *Wills*. They would have their Desires submitted to by others. . . .[4]

So that, Locke adds: 'Children who live together often strive for mastery, whose Wills shall carry it over the rest'; and if education did not intervene to correct this violent desire, they would seek to dominate those who are their inferiors in strength or in power, displaying, for example, insolence and contempt towards servants.

Locke's perception of the infant is certainly closer to the one offered by Saint Augustine at the beginning of the *Confessions* (or the one Melanie Klein was to theorize) than to the idea of the child put forward by Rousseau in *Émile*, only sixty years after Locke. Rousseau, who was familiar with Locke's work on the education of children, elaborates some of his views but departs from them on a cardinal point. For him, natural man is unaffected by original sin, for the very good reason that in his view, the 'original sin' is the shift to the social state – the shift which makes progress possible for human beings but, at the same time, denatures and estranges them. There is wickedness in 'man-made man', but there is none in man as he issued from God's hands. Émile is not corrupted by the desire to exist in the eyes of others. The healthy self-love [*amour de soi*] with which he is endowed therefore has nothing to do with the love of self [*amour-propre*] whose virulence was stigmatized by the Augustinians. 'It has no necessary relation to others' – this is the key sentence. Since his being is not entangled in relations with others, Émile neither thinks nor acts in connection with them; he could therefore harbour no ill will towards them.[5] Like Robinson Crusoe, Émile illustrates the dream of being oneself, as is the one God, *without having any necessary relations to others* – a dream which, far from corresponding to reality, attests instead to our desire for self-idealization in order to escape reality.

My proposed answer to the question of the inner springs of malice rests on three theses. These have been progressively imposed upon me through my work as a researcher and my involvement in the scientific community, as well as in the course of my psychoanalytic development, and lastly, quite simply, through my experience of life. Since this experience is common to all of us, I have cause to hope that the reader will find something familiar, even something personal, in my three propositions. I shall give a very brief introduction to them here (it is the book as a whole which makes them meaningful, illustrating them and drawing out their implications).

1. *Our sense that we exist is not given to us in advance, and once and for all.* We all know from experience that our awareness of ourselves is sometimes accompanied by a sense of nonexistence (with different shades of feeling, such as sadness, powerlessness, emptiness). This feeling can be brought about through humiliation, failure or envy; through resentment, isolation, depression, illness, a deterioration in our living conditions or the loss of someone close, and so on. Our sense of existing is so vulnerable that we feel the need to persuade ourselves that it is not so. This is why ideas with some philosophical or religious basis will always be at a premium when they shore up belief in a 'self' or a 'subject' that is not fashioned from the same stuff as life in society, but is 'natural', 'transcendent', and independent of our relations with others.

2. *The question of existing brings us into confrontation with others.* We not only have dealings with others once we exist, and whenever we are asked questions of either a practical or a moral nature. We have dealings with them in our being, and, as it were, even before we

exist (it is first of all in the mind of his or her parents that the baby exists as a person). And duration – the dimension within which our consciousness of ourselves extends – would not be formed or maintained if it did not assume a place within the much vaster ensemble of social time, and if it were not lived out in conjunction with the inner duration of other people. This is why, were we to occupy no place in anyone else's mind, our own mental space would empty out and wither away like a plant torn out of the soil which gave it sustenance.

3. *The desire which impels us to exist and to be fulfilled has no bounds.* This is one hypothesis which is easily advanced (it is almost an established fact) but remains hard to explain. Having awareness of ourselves implies simultaneously that we perceive what surrounds us from our own point of view, and that we place these perceptions in the framework of our own representations (for example, by situating a present event in relation to the inner thread of our memories and our anticipations). Our body, therefore, is not just a given quantity of matter occupying a small portion of space; it is the abode of a whole – a whole that forms the experience of itself within the invisible dimension of time, an experience which, as a consequence, is radically different from that of the visible world. As Longinus says in his treatise *On the Sublime*: 'Nature has distinguished man, as a creature of no mean or ignoble quality . . . thus within the scope of human enterprise there lie such powers of contemplation and thought that even the whole universe cannot satisfy them, but our ideas often pass beyond the limits that enring us.'[6] How could a whole be a part? A whole, inevitably, exceeds boundaries. Our suffering from being finite is therefore equally our suffering from being infinite. These observations seem to connect back to commonplace ideas: some metaphysical or religious feeling, some nostalgia for the ideal. Not a bit of it. We shall see, in fact, that the ideal of the infinite is only an infinite which is tamed, harnessed and made palatable, and that radical limitlessness is made manifest not in sweet dreams, but in the void of a bottomless well and the nightmare of destruction – as if the vital energy which animates the human body, once extended into psychic energy, were all at once to inhabit some absolute and limitless expanse. This is

abyssal narcissism, imaginary boundlessness, but its very real pressure is exerted upon each and every one of us, for better or for worse – a pressure which, let us be clear, is not reducible to biological impulses; there is a biological aggressiveness in man[7] (notably in young males), but malice does not boil down to this.

Coexisting in order to exist, needing others in order to be and to be oneself, is a necessity; but it is also an endless problem which has no satisfactory solution. Certainly, ways of being, modes of living and social mediations enable the mutual maintenance of the sense of existing; contrary to what is suggested by the Augustinian current, kindness, sociability, benevolence and goodness are not meaningless words. But, contrary to what well-intentioned humanism would have us believe, making room for others spontaneously, and ending up squeezed between narrow limits as a result, is not a natural process. Certainly, mutual love and recognition, 'being enriched by our differences', is wonderful. But that does not mean that there are not still times when – not to put too fine a point on it – other people piss us off.

If, in fact, my consciousness of myself is a consciousness of the world as spreading outwards away from me as its limitlessly radiating centre; if, at the same time, the mere fact that other people also exist means that my own sense of existing always remains limited in comparison with this immense horizon (to put it differently: if desire is not matched by any object which will truly fulfil it); if, finally, my sense of existing is dependent upon these others who are indispensable (being therefore relative and vulnerable), then the springs of hatred and malice are present within me and within each one of us: the springs of a revolt against the limitations implicit in coexistence, and a propensity to take it out on someone else (if only by making him or her aware of my bad mood). Thus, the force which impels us to exist encounters other people simultaneously as a condition of our existence and as an obstacle; at the root of all malice, however banal, there is therefore the desire for an omnipotence which will sweep away the obstacle and give us unconditional sway. In Kant's view, human malice is nothing more than the propensity to set love of self before moral principles.[8] Such a definition falls wide of the mark; wickedness does not come down just to egoism and lack of thought for others. On the contrary, it attacks them. Other people are always-already there on our horizon, and even the fact of ignoring them is an action, the action of pushing them aside – one way of reacting to their inevitable existence. Sade, who had doubtless given somewhat more thought to wickedness than Kant did, was emphatic on this point: what excites the libertine is being the cause of someone else's misery; this, I would add, is feeling oneself exist inside the other, in his place, by means of the suffering which prevents *him* from existing. Conversely, my own difficulty in existing impels me to perceive some other person as *someone who exists in my place* and whom, as a result, I hate, I envy, I am jealous of.

Malice, as we can see, is comprehensible insofar as it affects what one might call *the subject of existence*. The *subject of knowledge* – that is to say, the individual for whom the experience of the self is enacted through reflection and educated understanding – is thereby delivered both from other people and from the risk of not existing; he thinks, therefore he is. The *subject of knowledge* escapes the torments of interdependence, and the mastery he enjoys through thought gives him the illusion of being-himself as something natural and stable. The rationalism of the Enlightenment made of this subject the model human being, which is yet another way of taking the dream for reality. For in reality, the *subject of knowledge* does not coincide with the universal; rather, it corresponds to one of the ways of being human. And ever since we have become ensconced in it, this particular 'posture' has prevented us from understanding malice.

This constitutes a serious obstacle. Is there any possible way round it? I have tried to find one by going back and forth between narrative and reflection. Indeed, the great advantage of fictional narratives is that they are not addressed to the *subject of knowledge*; in a story there is always someone at loggerheads with someone else, and someone who is a prey to disorder, immoderation, or some other way of going beyond acceptable bounds. Stories speak to us about the *subject of existence*, and it is this which they address. Moreover, people consume fictional narratives through reading, going to the cinema or watching television, activities which are undertaken much less for the sake of knowledge than for experiencing pleasure or, at least, avoiding boredom.

Although they do not fall into the category of education, the scenes in a narrative and their sequence are still eloquent. This is why, if we are able to learn something from a dream we have had, we can likewise learn something from a story which has made a strong impression on us – the great difference between the dream and the fictional narrative being that the former concerns one person, whereas the latter concerns thousands, even millions, of people.[9]

The task of discerning ourselves in the mysterious mirror held out to us by fictional narratives is not an easy one. There is indeed a great temptation to interpret the story on the basis of some scholarly knowledge we possess and, consequently, to assimilate it to that knowledge and, thus, learn nothing new from it. This also spares us from having to recognize ourselves in the possibly unpleasant image which the mirror shows us. In *The Interpretation of Dreams*, Freud wagers instead that *his dreams 'know' something about him which he does not know himself.* This is the fundamental principle which I have striven to follow. I have therefore considered that what made me interested in certain stories of evil-doing resided not merely in the stories themselves, *but also in me.* For even if they had been read attentively and analysed methodically, they would have taught me nothing about malice had I not been prepared for them to tell me something in the first place about my own maliciousness.[10] In fact it is not possible to think about wickedness without confronting some degree of repression. What a narrative says about the *subject of existence* is something that the *subject of knowledge* is not in a position to hear.

So what I had to do was ask myself about the impressions made by the story, about the invisible connection formed between the scenes which had struck me and the way in which I myself exist. Then it was a question of attempting to formulate something about this connection, this resonance; and finally, of comparing these first formulations with ideas which I have – which we have – about what a human being is (the story itself sometimes makes reference to these ideas, but they are not necessarily at one with the 'thoughts' which its narrative thread obscurely weaves). So it was a matter not of boiling the story down to reason, but of making it suggest its own reasons to me, and thus provide me with a genuine *philosophical tool.*

This way of proceeding is a kind of extension of the psychoanalytic experience; it appeals to the type of sensibility whose development this experience encourages. Psychoanalysis, moreover, touches precisely on realities which concern the inner springs of malice. In the pages which follow, however, I do not make *explicit* reference to the concepts elaborated by Freud and Lacan. Since psychoanalytic theory was elaborated on the basis of clinical experience, and in order to give an account of this experience, whenever psychoanalytic language ceases to engage (or to grapple) with clinical events, it loses its evocative power and its bite. It is even in danger (as it's application to realities which are foreign to the clinical has shown only too well) of turning into a screen on which the patterns have become so familiar that they hide events rather than give access to them. Now, what I am striving to share with the reader is above all the human reality to which certain stories of evil-doing have given me access. Thus, for those of my readers who are accustomed to thinking within the framework of psychoanalytic theory, I have seen fit to leave it up to them to make associations here and there between the concepts of psychoanalysis and the words I use. As for the other readers, at least I shall have avoided interposing between them and the evocation of events a conceptual framework which, paradoxically, would here have risked contributing to the repression of those events rather than to their emergence in the field of reflection.

Why, out of sundry narratives of evil-doing, have I chosen Mary Shelley's novel *Frankenstein*, published in 1818, as the pivot of this essay? The main reason is obviously subjective: this story made an impression on me, and more than any other it has stimulated my thoughts on malice. The objective reason came later. In *Frankenstein* the two currents I mentioned above, Augustinianism and Enlightenment humanism, combine and intersect. The latter manifests itself most of all in the ideas which run through the narrative. For all that they were Romantics, Mary and her husband, the poet Percy Bysshe Shelley, were equally ardent disciples of William Godwin,

Mary's father, a classic Enlightenment man. Thus, in many respects, *Frankenstein* is anchored in eighteenth-century philosophy. This novel has often been read in the light of ideas and intentions which contemporary interpreters have seen fit to attribute to the author – usually rational ideas and praiseworthy intentions which are approved of and shared by the interpreter. Read within this perspective, the novel obviously has little to teach us about malice. What the presence of Enlightenment thought in *Frankenstein* can help us to understand, on the other hand, is the reason why we find it so difficult nowadays to think about malice. For, by combining with the *story*, the novel's *ideas* reorder the violence in such a way that it appears to be in accordance with humanist and progressive conceptions. In reality, however, the deployment of violence in the story is nonetheless in keeping with the concatenation of its events. The story ought therefore to be considered in itself, and carefully distinguished from the logic of the *ideas*. The level of *narration*, which is governed by a destructive chain of events, takes its place in the Augustinian current. The fact is that, beyond its kinship with the Gothic novel, *Frankenstein* owes a great deal to Milton's *Paradise Lost*, which mounts an extraordinary Augustinian *mise en scène* of wickedness.

The subtitle of *Frankenstein* is *The Modern Prometheus*. This reference to Prometheus is, at heart, ambiguous – first, because it refers as much to the 'creator' (Victor Frankenstein) as to his 'creature' (the monster); second, because it also bears the imprint of the two currents: the novel is Promethean inasmuch as it participates in the modern ideal of individual political emancipation; but it is simultaneously anti-Promethean, since it stages the catastrophic effects of the immoderation which animates the characters. *Frankenstein*, as I shall show at the end of this volume, thus offers us an opportunity to reflect on the ambiguities of the Western ideal of emancipation – an ideal which, on the one hand, is based on unquestionable forms of knowledge and progress, and efficiently promotes their development; but which, from another point view, goes hand in hand with a certain presumption regarding the power to be oneself, and a degree of blindness about the inner source of malice.

Blindness about the inner springs of malice is expressed within contemporary ideology through the persistence of the old dualist tradition (albeit in a recycled and modified form), whose emergence Norman Cohn has skilfully traced back as far as Zarathustra in his book *Cosmos, Chaos and the World to Come*.[11] The story of Adam and Eve as it has been interpreted by Christianity offers us a familiar image of this dualism. Man is good when he issues from the hands of God. Evil derives from a principle which is inherent neither in God nor in man's original nature; evil entered humanity by way of sin and the Devil. Modern secular thought has not attempted to reinterpret this myth, nor to strip it of the dualist guise in which it was attired by Christianity. Since the Church presented it as a historical fact, modern thought did no more than deny this (hard to resist, given the highly unlikely nature of that story about the apple). But when it rejected original sin, modern thought did not reject dualism. Instead, it upheld it by recasting the myth: Adam's original state was extended to all of humankind; as for the serpent, it was replaced by another form of external evil: the work of a tyrannical, unjust and corrupt society, or of some malign ideology. Thus became established the belief whereby human beings are capable of living on good terms with one another if only they have a wholesome education that will help them to be at one with their rational nature. Of course, it does happen that Evil (which is by definition inhuman and incomprehensible) creeps into them in some pernicious way to wreak its havoc (Nazism, totalitarianism, racism, etc.); nevertheless, since this Evil is not inherent in them, one can hope to eradicate it.

Although it is unrealistic, this belief, this wishful thinking, is still shared by the best minds of our day. It has not, however, succeeded entirely in stifling good sense, and here and there we find critiques of the dualism which blithely frees us from acknowledging the bad wishes within ourselves, encouraging us to project them outside us. Tzvetan Todorov, for instance, deplores the repeated division between us (the good) and them (the bad): 'One precept for the century ahead might be: ... not fighting evil in the name of good, but ... Manichaean thought itself.'[12] Alain Finkielkraut, for his part, makes a critique of Ernest Renan's presumptuous statement: 'I, being educated, cannot find evil in myself'. This is an affirmation which goes hand in hand with the customary dualistic scenario: good will triumph over evil in the end – we must enlighten the people, and humankind will be delivered from evil.[13]

In short, if we are to escape from foolish orthodoxies and face up to human malice, we must leave behind dualistic thinking. We must, yes, but how? This is where we run into two substantial difficulties.

The first difficulty is that our tradition of thought is closely bound up with monotheism, and is ill equipped for elaborating a non-dualist conception of human beings – that is to say, a conception that would allow us to understand *how what is good and what is bad in us are connected to the same root, deep within us and, as a consequence, impossible to extirpate.* For this reason, in Chapter 1 I shall go back to the time before monotheism in order to show how the cosmogonies of the eastern Mediterranean offered a much more fertile context than our own for thinking about wickedness. The logic which animated these ancient cosmogonies has become alien to us; therefore the reader might find it absurd or irrelevant. None the less, it is in fact a very simple logic, and one which, once understood, turns out to be extremely useful for understanding how the human psyche becomes constructed on the basis of a fount of limitlessness which, while it is the source of a vital and beneficial energy, also opens the door to supremely destructive wishes.

The second obstacle is even harder to surmount than the first. 'Manichaean temptation and egocentric illusion ['it is the other, not I, who is malicious'] are bound up with our most intimate inclinations, notes Todorov.[14] As I suggested above, the sense of existing is unfortunately not a fundamental possession provided for us by nature, and in sufficient quantity; we are also constantly required to supplement it. This is something we do primarily by maintaining an idea of ourselves which is as favourable as possible. It is painful in the first place to acknowledge errors, deficiencies, failings or desires which contradict norms; but it is even more painful to realize that we are a prey to truly destructive feelings (this is why, in the course of the psychoanalytic cure, the patient's discovery of the hatred he or she harbours is often more frightening than the discovery of unavowed sexual desires; this is also why a destructive wish can contrive to be smuggled in under cover of a sexual fantasy which can be assumed – not to say claimed outright – by someone who is independently minded).

I am aware that this book's invitation to face up to this double obstacle demands a lot of the reader. If the difficulty turns out to be insurmountable, the book will have been of no use whatsoever (other than to confirm that the propensity to dodge the fact of human malice and replace it with an Evil that is as inhuman as it is absolute still has a lot of life in it). But some readers, I am sure, will follow the example given to us by Milton, who, instead of demonizing his fellow men, as we tend to do, was able to see a human soul in Satan.

1

The Price of Monotheism

'And the Lord said unto Satan, Hast thou considered my servant Job, that there is none like him in the earth, a perfect and an upright man, one that feareth God, and escheweth evil?' Satan objects that Yahweh has showered Job with gifts: 'But put forth thine hand now, and touch all that he hath, and he will curse thee to thy face.'[1] Let it be so, replies Yahweh, and soon Job is so overwhelmed with wretchedness that in the end he exclaims: 'Let the day perish wherein I was born!'

Three of Job's friends come to comfort him. They see that he is covered with boils from head to toe, and that he is deeply downcast. They urge him to keep his trust in Yahweh. But Job continues to complain about the unjust sufferings which afflict him, and which strike down so many other innocent people. To his friends' horror, Job claims that he is wronged by God. Out of the depths of his distress he reproaches Yahweh for a silence which adds to his injustice: 'I cry unto thee, and thou dost not hear me.'

Finally, Yahweh himself addresses Job. Yahweh gives no answer whatsoever to his questionings about justice, but he crushes Job's insolence by emphasizing at length just how much the immensity and power of the universe which he has created exceed him. Job answers: 'I know that thou canst do every thing . . . I have heard of thee by the hearing of the ear: but now mine eye seeth thee. Wherefore I abhor myself, and repent in dust and ashes.'

And Yahweh restores Job to his former state.

The Book of Job dates from the fifth century before Christ. Other texts have been found on clay tablets; they are Mesopotamian and were written between the end of the third millennium and the beginning of the first; as in the Book of Job, in these texts a man asks himself what wrong he can have committed to have fallen prey to such sickness, sorrow and impoverishment.[2] In the period before the second half of the third millennium, the Mesopotamians explained these things as attacks by evil demons. Later, however, the answer was to be found in the faults of the complainer: he had done something wrong; he had unknowingly offended a god; now he had to wait for the god's wrath to be appeased, and for things to turn out better. At the beginning of the first millennium, however, the complainer does not confine himself to his own case; he extends his question to humanity as a whole, and stigmatizes social injustice. If we confront the problem of evil in these terms, the answers seem somewhat inadequate: human beings must persevere with good behaviour and will be rewarded for it; in any case, divine plans will be beyond their understanding, and the gods are not directly responsible for evil. In the Book of Job, the chasm between the question asked and its answer has become even deeper.

First, because we know from the outset that Job has done nothing, either deliberately or unwittingly, to offend Yahweh; he is genuinely innocent.

Secondly, because Yahweh does not answer Job's question 'Why?'. It is as if, once Job stands before him, Yahweh says: '*Hier ist kein warum*', 'There is no why here' – the answer Primo Levi received, after arriving at the Monowitz concentration camp, in reply to his '*Warum?*'.[3]

Lastly, because, in order to silence Job, Yahweh affirms his omnipotence; he cannot therefore refuse responsibility for the evil brought down upon someone or something other than himself.

Thus, ever since Job, all those who believe in a God who is one and individual have found themselves exposed to a question without an answer: in the face of the evils which overwhelm human beings, in the face of the sufferings which they inflict upon one another, how does one acknowledge the existence of a God who does as he wishes and simultaneously wishes good? This is a question without an answer because no one, Christians without exception, is con-vinced by the explanation which the story of original sin is supposed to provide. There are obviously only two solutions.

Either one gives up picturing the divine being in the guise of an individual God. God does not exist: 'There is Auschwitz, therefore there can be no God' was the conclusion reached by Primo Levi at the end of his interview with Ferdinando Camon.[4] The divine being could not be a person; this is the traditional notion in China.[5]

Or one puts limits on God's powers. This is how, in *Le concept de Dieu après Auschwitz*,[6] the philosopher Hans Jonas supports the idea that God is not in fact omnipotent. But already, in Antiquity, Greeks who believed in a single God acknowledged that this God bowed before the nature of things. Moses, Galen wrote in the second century after Jesus Christ, 'thinks that for God all is possible . . .; but we [the Greeks] do not judge it to be so; we affirm that there are things which by their nature are impossible'.[7]

In fact, for the majority of people today, the 'problem of evil' is no longer a theological but a practical one: it is a matter of concrete remedies to be applied to the evils suffered by humanity. Having done with the theological question of evil, however, is one thing; thinking about the inner springs of malice is another! What is important here is to make the distinction between the two questions quite clear:

- *Is the existence of a God who is one and individual, just and infinite, and therefore all-powerful, compatible with the world as it is?* This is the 'problem of evil'.
- *Is the notion of the infinite in itself compatible with notions of justice and goodness?* This is the problem of the inner springs of malice.

Just as the terms of the first question are very familiar to us, so the terms of the second, as I have just formulated them, are largely unfamiliar. The aim of this chapter will therefore be to clarify them.

In his initial state, *created in God's own image*, man could only be good. By proposing to 'regenerate' this original man, Enlighten-ment philosophy and the revolutionary currents were therefore preserving a precious part of the Christian conception of human beings. The first task to be accomplished in order to rethink the question of human wickedness is to interrogate this 'progress' which is manifest in Job's story: the idea of an individual God is both infinite and good. What will be of more precise interest to us is this: while polytheism makes it possible to conceive of justice (or goodness) and omnipotence as separate qualities, monotheism, on the other hand, is compelled to synthesize them. And it is this impossible synthesis which gives rise to the confusion that prevents us from thinking about the inner springs of malice. Let us try, therefore, to sketch out a little 'archaeology' or 'deconstruction' of the one God's omnipotence.

Omnipotence is the attribute of a person, not a thing. An example will help us to see this more clearly. Moses is preparing to climb Mount Sinai to receive the Law from the mouth of Yahweh.

> And it came to pass on the third day in the morning, that there were thunders and lightnings, and a thick cloud upon the mount, and the voice of the trumpet exceeding loud; so that all the people that was in the camp trembled. . . . And Mount Sinai was altogether on a smoke, because the Lord descended upon it in fire: and the smoke thereof ascended as the smoke of a furnace, and the whole mount quaked greatly. . . . And all the people saw the thunderings, and the lightnings, and the noise of the trumpet, and the mountain smoking: and when the people saw it, they removed, and stood afar off. . . . Let not God speak with us, lest we die. . . . And the sight of the glory of the Lord was like devouring fire on the top of the mount.[8]

These descriptions evoke a volcanic eruption, a destructive and terrifying force. However, this is not to say that Mount Sinai, the site of these spectacular phenomena, is itself omnipotent. It is Yahweh who, through these phenomena, transmits his omnipotence to the people of Israel (to be more precise, it is the author of the text who leads us to imagine divine omnipotence). Likewise, faced with huge waves lashing in the midst of a violent storm, one would describe them as extraordinarily powerful, but not all-powerful.

One can also say that the sight of them provokes a sense of omnipotence – either because one imagines that God is their author, or because one identifies with their seething fury.

How does divine being come to be represented in the form of a person, and how does this person become one alone and, as a result, infinite and all-powerful? In order to answer these questions, we shall have to follow two central strands: one leads from the child–parent relationship to man's relation with God; the other leads from gods who form part of the world to a Creator who is external to this world.

One of the difficulties we have to confront as we move away from childhood is the difficulty of living in a world without parents. Since our first steps in life are possible only through the guidance of these providential divinities, it is not surprising that we should be tempted to find replacements for them, either on earth or in heaven. If those beings who take the place of our parents give us a sense of security, even when we fear them, equally – insofar as they are idealized – they inspire a feeling of trust, a feeling which our parents, or those who are actually close to us, unfortunately do not always allow us to experience. We need to trust someone, to trust life – it's good for us. The idealization of parents, the family line, or some authority which takes over from them, maintains in us a sense of our existence and our value.

As we read the Bible, it is easy to see that Yahweh is in certain respects a Super-Parent. First because the Covenant is a fictive forming of kinship.[9] Then, because the bond with Yahweh is exclusive, preventing the Hebrews from making a similar parental connection with any other god. The populations which surround them have their own protector gods, rather as each child has his or her own parents in the playground of a nursery school; when a quarrel breaks out between two children, their parents, although they are absent, exert an invisible form of protection. In the turmoil of conflict, they find reassurance in taunting one other: 'My dad's bigger and stronger than yours.' This is exactly the recourse that Yahweh guarantees to the children of Israel[10] – on condition, of course, that they are faithful and obedient to Him. This is a condition which gives prophets a chance to play their own part. The prophet behaves like a big brother among small children; in the absence of the parents, he exercises delegated authority in their name. In this guise, as Michael Walzer points out, prophets rise up against the oppression of the weak by the strong;[11] in God's eyes, as in the eyes of an impartial father, all his children are equal. Simultaneously, however, prophets enjoy the superior power which they attribute to Yahweh, and they allow it to erupt in their diatribes: if the children are naughty, Super-Parent will bring down dreadful punishments upon them; if they keep faith with the Covenant, he will instead give them the strength to exterminate their enemies (the Hebrews' neighbours are obviously no more lenient: it is written in the chronicles of an Assyrian monarch that, having taken the citadel of Hullaya, 'I cast upon the fire and burned the three thousand inhabitants whom I had taken prisoner, without leaving a single one as hostage'[12]).

One prophet in particular, Jonah, cannot hide the fact that he was looking forward to enjoying the destruction which Yahweh had given him the task of announcing. The writer of the pages devoted to this prophet demonstrates what might be humour, and what is at any rate a critical viewpoint, when he depicts a Jonah piqued by the pardon Yahweh grants to the inhabitants of Nineveh. But the story of Jonah sent by Yahweh to Nineveh, the capital of the Assyrian Empire, is equally instructive as clear evidence that by now Super-Parent reigns over a much-extended family: he is no longer just the god of Israel; the Assyrians, too, owe him obedience. In the eighth century BC, the prophets move on from what is called henotheism to monotheism. Yahweh was stronger than the other gods. Now that he is the one and only, he is truly all-powerful (and speaking in His Name is even more gratifying).

Yahweh is not just the partner in the Covenant, he is also the origin of order in the world. In this guise, too, his power is an issue, but not in the same way as in his role as providential Super-Parent. The question of the plurality of the gods also comes up, but not in the same terms as in the case of the god of the Covenant.

In shaping their idea of the formation of the world, the

Hebrews, as we know, borrowed considerably from their prede-
cessors established in Canaan or Palestine.[13] Like the Egyptians
and the Mesopotamians, they did not conceive of a creation *ex
nihilo*, a recent and original notion. They were more interested in
the order of the world and the process of formation whereby this
order came about. Within this perspective, creation narratives
could obviously take cognizance of various ordering powers, each
of them reigning over its own domain. Even when these narratives
gave importance to a single Orderer, this power was not omnipotent. In the beginning, there is Limitlessness, Chaos, the Abyss,
the Great Tumult. The defined and finite being which rises out of
this non-being must, in its turn, set limits and divisions upon it, an
order which makes it habitable. This is quite a tall order, as the
story is told in the *Enuma Elish*, the Mesopotamian epic in which
we see Marduk confront Tiamat, the mother-monster of the abyss.
Likewise, the Baal revealed by the Ras-Shamra excavations has to
vanquish a monstrous serpent named Leviathan. And likewise, the
God of Israel breaks the heads of Leviathan in pieces before separating day from night.[14]

According to these ancient creation stories, *it is only non-being
which exists absolutely or infinitely.* Beings – among them a god or gods
– exist at the cost of a definition, a demarcation; it is therefore
impossible to be simultaneously perfect and infinite; it is impossible
to be simultaneously just (guaranteeing order) and all-powerful
(divine power resembles that of a monarch: it is the power of
controlling other powers). These speculations would be of no value
to us if they aimed only to give an account of the formation of the
material world. But they also constitute a way of conceiving of the
social and psychic world; as Marc Augé says: 'cosmogony is also a
form of anthropogeny'.[15] For this reason, our interest in them is
justified.

Ideas akin to these mythical speculations had not yet become
foreign to a philosopher such as Aristotle, who also made a distinction between the perfect and the limitless. However, Jewish monotheism and, in Greece, Platonism, had long since begun to
undermine these ideas and replace them with an altogether different system of thought. We could even say that the transformation

has its origins in Greece in the first half of the fifth century with
Parmenides, for whom the existence of the non-being which is
Chaos is a matter of scandal for logical thought:

> Nor shall I let thee say or think that it came from what is not;
> For it cannot be said or thought that 'it is not'.[16]

If primordial limitlessness does not exist, being does not have to
come into being, it does not have to differentiate itself from Chaos;
being is in the beginning, therefore it is not limited by anything.
Parmenides' poem and the Book of Job are contemporaries; both
of them mark the disappearance of Chaos and the coming of the
Being as simultaneously One and above alteration. The two onsets
of being to which each of these texts corresponds meet in the
culture of the Hellenized Jews, and their association will continue
into Christianity. The new conception of the world and of human
beings of which these two texts mark the beginning entails a
splitting between the level of immanence and the level of transcendence: the Being remains identical unto himself, the material world
is subject to alteration; God is no longer part of the world, the
world is his creation.

In the Book of Job, Leviathan is therefore no longer the fearsome fount of matter and energy that pre-existed Yahweh; instead,
Yahweh presents the forces of Chaos as having been created by
Himself. Certainly, Yahweh still preserves some of the characteristics
of the god who stems the limitless, who divides and organizes a pre-
existing Chaos by deploying powers which are not radically transcendent in relation to those over which his actions take place.
Thus Yahweh points out to Job that it was He 'who shut up the sea
with doors, when it brake forth, as if it had issued out of the womb'.
But Yahweh also presents altogether different characteristics, and it
is the new Yahweh, the new conception of the world, which is by far
the more developed: Yahweh gives a lengthy description of Behemoth and Leviathan, the two monsters who once embodied the
pre-existing abyss and limitlessness of the fresh and salt waters.
Yahweh evokes their power, and their power is His, for these
monsters are now his creatures.

Behold now Behemoth, which I
made with thee; he eateth grass as an ox.
Lo now, his strength is in his loins,
and his force is in the navel of his belly.
He moveth his tail like a cedar:
the sinews of his stones are wrapped together.
His bones are as strong pieces of brass;
his bones are like bars of iron.
He is the chief of the ways of God . . .
Canst thou draw out Leviathan with a hook?
Or his tongue with a cord which thou lettest down?
. . .
Shall not one be cast down even at the sight of him?
None is so fierce that dare stir him up:
who then is able to stand before me?
Who hath prevented me, that I should repay him?
Whatsoever is under the whole heaven is mine.
. . .
Upon earth there is not his like,
who is made without fear.[17]

Contrary to what the old creation stories narrated, no one here
has had to fight Behemoth or Leviathan, not even Yahweh. The
latter (who designates himself by the name El) has no need to
confront them, since he himself created them. Thus, the omnipotence which he now enjoys feeds upon these monsters of Chaos:
these entities from which there once emanated a terrible power of
destruction but also of inexhaustible resources, so that they had to
be simultaneously held back and drawn upon, these entities are
now called to bear witness to divine Omnipotence. As they are thus
absorbed by the one God, the ambivalence which characterized
them becomes progressively effaced. Of course, Yahweh remains
fearsome, but that is not to say that God is the same as primordial
limitlessness, that is to say, simultaneously good and evil. God is
goodness; evil is outside God. And if God is goodness, the infinite –
and, consequently, omnipotence – can no longer be ambivalent:
they are forms of perfection.

In a text entitled 'Le message universel de la Bible' (The Universal Message of the Bible[18]), Jean Bottéro presents access to monotheism as an 'incomparable progress'. This, in certain respects, contains a prejudice, one which is obviously very widespread in countries with a monotheistic culture (but one with which Chinese culture, for example, is in complete disagreement). For all the value of monotheism's contribution (that promotion of the individual, of the 'subject', of which Western intellectuals are so proud), we must nevertheless beware of regarding it as an *absolute* progress. It is oversimplifying things to say that with the shift from polytheism (or paganism) to monotheism, man reaches a truer conception of himself. Just as we talk about 'the price of progress', we must also talk about the price of monotheism.

What does this price consist of? What went before it prepared us to understand it. The old conception of the world and of human beings made it possible to conceive of the ambivalence of an initial fount of limitlessness: destructive in that there was nothing to limit it, but a source of life inasmuch as it entered into a process of differentiation; non-being whose expansion had to be held back, but also a resource which could be drawn upon. The *dualism* which succeeded this *duality* does not offer the same possibilities for thought. It no longer makes it possible to consider the fundamentally destructive character of the infinite; and it no longer makes it possible to think of how the performance of a good action brings about, in addition to the will for good, an energy which, taken by itself, would be destructive.

With the opposition between good and evil, the Devil and God Almighty, the ambivalence in the fount of limitlessness is, so to speak, dismantled. The infinite, toned down and idealized, becomes God's, while destructiveness and confusion become Satan's (until enlightened thought makes Satan himself disappear). In certain respects, Satan arises out of Chaos; he exerts the seductiveness of what is limitless, he transgresses all boundaries, all limits, he is a power of the night which, unnoticed, creeps into souls. But when Chaos becomes diabolical, it ceases in the same moment to be split between what is to be taken and what is to be left in order that what is can be formed.

We shall see how, in Milton's *Paradise Lost*, Satan appears necessarily against a background of Chaos and the Abyss, against a background of an infinite non-being which is the external reflection of his own interiority. But Milton's Satan is not orthodox. Beyond those features which connect him to an Augustinian vision of the depths of the human soul, he preserves something of the Titan (it may be that even when it aims to be Christian, as is the case with Milton's work, literature can never altogether break with a pagan vision of human beings). This is why this figure's limitlessness transmits to him an energy before whose depiction readers of Milton experience a kind of happiness, because this picture kindles in them a sense of their own vitality; thanks to Milton's Satan, readers can discover, deep within their own bad feelings, something that is good, strong and alive.

Monotheistic orthodoxy, however, closes off access to this ambivalence: Satan is the point of origin of what should not have been; he is there to confirm that only evil can come from the fount of limitlessness which underlies desire. This is why, from the point when the story of Adam and Eve would be taken over by dualist thought (that is to say, roughly from when Philo of Alexandria gave it a Platonist interpretation in the first century AD), it would be said that Satan himself, in the guise of the cunning serpent, tempted our first parents. Because of the dualism which was then superimposed on the very ancient myth of Genesis, eating the forbidden fruit no longer brought our first parents any benefits. From then on, the story of Adam and Eve will have no other function but to explain the origin of *what should not have been.*

Egyptian, Greek and Mesopotamian creation stories (including what has survived of them in the Bible) did not derive from a dualist conception; and they did not speak of Chaos as what should not have been. They said that Chaos should not reign alone, they said that being is formed by differentiation, by keeping itself at some distance from the original limitlessness. Chaos is not, like Satan, a radical evil; it is the bedrock of the world and of human beings, it is the sum of the potentialities from which what is can be, it is the limitless energy which, so long as it is contained by forms, can nourish the dynamism of life. Marduk organizes the world by drawing upon the matter provided for him by the body of Tiamat. In Egypt, the first differentiated existence – a hill, an egg or a lotus – emerges from the primordial ocean; it separates from it, but it has its source in it. Likewise, in Hesiod's *Theogony*, the ordered and habitable world is built upon the basis of a tension between the resources and threats of a primordial Chaos on the one hand, and the processes of separation, distancing and differentiation on the other. Therefore good does not come from the One, but from a process which involves a duality. On the basis of these pagan conceptions (which are not so far from those elaborated by Chinese thought), it is possible to imagine the construction of the human psyche in terms of the formation of the world. It is possible to conceive of it as being ambivalent by nature, not because of a fall, an evil by which it has become contaminated. Thinking of human beings as being divided within themselves by nature, and therefore in their very being, is not at all the same thing as thinking of them as being divided because of an event which is indeed decisive, but leaves the one and indivisible kernel of their being intact.

Thus, monotheism has not just provided a framework that is favourable to the emancipation of the individual, it has also incited him or her to see, in the image fashioned of God as singular and unique, an ideal prototype for the self. The movement of secularization which has transformed Europe since the end of the Middle Ages certainly has meant an emancipation from the Church's guardianship. But what this movement sees less readily when it tells itself its own story is that it has also meant a deepening of Christianity. With its reference to man in a state of nature, Enlightenment philosophy prolongs the Christian vision of the original man made in the image of God. Thus, in the wake of the theologians, it acknowledges something of the infinite in human beings. But even more than for the theologians, this limitlessness has by this point lost its violent and transgressive character, and is reduced to a legitimate kinship between divine perfection and human will and reason.

To conclude, let us return to the Book of Job, so that we can interrogate the precise relationship established between the creature and his Creator. In the Book of Job, Yahweh appears not as

one of the gods revered by the peoples who surrounded the
Hebrews, gods which were powers that *were part* of the universe.
Man and God are now separated by an infinite distance. Yet,
paradoxically, a new intimacy brings them closer. In fact, according
to the Christian (and, more particularly, the Protestant) interpretation, Job accedes to a new dimension of himself; stripped of
everything that attached him to this world, cast down by his fall, Job
would finally touch the inner truth of his being. He would achieve
truth by surrendering himself to faith, faith in the singular and
omnipotent Being who, beyond this world, would be the source of
his own being.

What inclines those who read the Book of Job to adhere to this
interpretation, and even to identify in some way with Job, is not
strictly speaking the *ideas* prompted by the dialogue between Job
and Yahweh, it is the *mise en scène* of the confrontation itself. When
we read the story of Job, and experience a feeling that a certain
truth is to be found within it, we are tempted to express this feeling
by connecting it to the question at issue in this story. How many
priests and pastors have thus been led to hark back to a series of
reflections about the 'question of evil' for the edification of their
faithful, and about acceptance, by virtue of faith itself, that there is
no answer to this question – an acceptance through which the soul
affirms its inmost self before the tragic and infinite gulf which
separates it from a reconciliation with what lies outside it. This kind
of argument fits well with the emotion stirred up by the story of
Job, thanks to the intensity of its *mise en scène*: the tragedy and the
pathos which cast a halo around the supposed access of the inner
self to its own truth seem to merge with this emotion. The fact that
the emotion is genuinely felt by the reader thus brings its guarantee
to the truth of the argument. This recuperation of affect by the
discourse which interprets it, however, is in no sense enough to
prove that the impression experienced by the reader is in fact due
to the causes ascribed to it by the interpretation. We should even
say that to some extent the interpretation mis-recognizes the
sources of the fascination exerted by the Book of Job across the
centuries.[19] Let us pause for a moment before this grandiose

picture: the confrontation between a man reduced to nothing and the fount of omnipotence from which the entire universe issues.

If Yahweh provides no justification in answer to Job's recriminations, it is obviously because the author of the poem himself has none to offer. But the author, instead of making do with vacant and dilatory replies such as the Mesopotamian texts would put forward – therein lies his genius – provides the reader with some compensation for the frustration attached to the scandal of evil and the absence of any justification. This compensation is a kind of satisfaction in which the painful annihilation into which Job is cast down is inverted.

If we wanted to translate this satisfaction into words, we would only have to paraphrase the thundering speech whereby Yahweh shatters Job's complaints, more or less like this: 'If you had not fallen into the abyss of suffering, you would never have come near to this satisfaction of seeing yourself at last in the mirror of the Almighty. When you were prosperous, your horizon did not extend beyond the relative well-being to which you connected your happiness. Now that you are nothing, at last you can possess an absolute fulfilment from which you were kept far away by the enjoyment of that well-being – a boundlessness truly without limits, since it combines the creative power of Yahweh with the destructive force of Leviathan.'

The best formulation of this satisfaction is, I believe, to be found in Herman Melville's novel *Moby Dick*. *Moby Dick* is rather like the Book of Job, but without all the theological disputation. Captain Ahab, tied to the singularly huge white whale that Melville compares to Leviathan, is Job crushed and conquered by the power of a God who has absorbed the forces of Chaos within himself. But this all-powerful monster who haunts the oceans of the globe is not named as God by Melville; he takes care not to reduce the richness of his novel to the univocity of a doctrine. This time the pleasure the reader derives from the confrontation between Ahab and Moby Dick remains open to the ambivalence which underlies it. This ambivalence is not masked by the superimposition of a discourse of truth which, in deifying omnipotence, passes it off as perfection;

whereas in the Book of Job, the discourse of truth which combines with the story exposes the reader to a fraudulent seduction.

The story of Job is that of a strange mirror-relation, that of the nothing with the all. There is an element of truth in this story: it is true that we are bound in some intimate and mysterious way to a fount of limitlessness. But the story, with its mirror-effect (which reinforces the Christian discourse of interpretation), exerts a seductiveness which distorts the truth; it inclines us to take this fount for the site of our true fulfilment, for an ultimate-self-being. It encourages us to believe that true self-being is rooted in the One. Hence a dualism: on the one hand Being; on the other its opposite, what cuts us off from it. Hence, too, the confusion of moral good with fulfilment. Hence, moreover, that hateful and cruel invention of the Last Judgement. While in reality, our being is formed both on the basis of a fount of limitlessness and on the basis of the limitations which cut us off from it. So that moral good, far from leading to fulfilment, demands that self-being make the best of incompleteness.

So, in order to think about wickedness and to distinguish it from goodness, we must simultaneously acknowledge that we are connected to that fount of limitlessness, and acknowledge its ambivalence. This is much more difficult than it seems, for it means accepting the unacceptable; accepting, as we lose a part of this fount, that we are condemned for ever to enjoy only a part of ourselves.

This conflict, which contains no real solution, covertly animates the discourses which have a bearing on what we are and what is to be accomplished. We can see this conflict at work in the bewildered fascination which the figure of Job has prompted in authors such as Edward Young, William Blake, Kierkegaard, Ballanche, Quinet, Lamartine, Hugo or Dostoevsky. Like other authors, Hugo linked Job and Prometheus, both of them in revolt against the arbitrariness of divine authority, and in his *Toilers of the Sea* the character of Gilliatt was meant to be 'a Job-Prometheus'.[20] Is it because Job stands up against injustice that he stands for the ideal I? Or is it not, rather, because in his confrontation with omnipotence he identifies with it? Does he represent suffering humanity? Does he

prefigure the redemptive calvary of the Just Man crucified? Probably
all of these put together. With, in the background, the fantasy of
pain inverted into pleasure, as is suggested by a passage from
Edmund Burke in which, in order to illustrate his conception of
the sublime, he quotes the Book of Job; a sublimity whose pleasure,
Burke explains, is prompted by representations of all-powerfulness,
therefore of destruction, terror and pain. 'The idea of pain, in its
highest degree, is much stronger than the highest degree of
pleasure,' he writes, for 'pain is always inflicted by a power in some
way superior.'[21]

In the twentieth century, we find Job associated with Auschwitz.
In a text entitled 'A Vision of Apocalypse',[22] Elie Wiesel points out
that there are certain texts which were not included in the sacred
canon because they were too impregnated with despair, and that
for this reason the Book of Job came close to being excised and
declared apocryphal. Within this perspective, the survivor of Auschwitz looks like a new Job. A victim, like him, of a destructive
omnipotence, he has lived through an experience which 'will for
ever defy any possible understanding'. In *La Nuit*, Wiesel, too,
presents himself as a Job in revolt: 'I was nothing more than ashes,
but I felt stronger than this Almighty to whom my life had been
bound for so long.'[23]

Primo Levi, too, became interested in Job. He imagines him no
longer before Yahweh, but before what he calls 'the dark hole' of
Auschwitz: 'Impoverished, bereft of his children, covered in boils,
Job sits among the pariahs scratching himself with a potsherd and
argues with God. It is an unequal argument. God the creator of
marvels and monsters crushes him beneath his omnipotence.'[24]

It is clear that with Auschwitz, omnipotence goes back whence it
came before it turned into God's prerogative: back to Chaos. Or
rather, it doesn't; it goes back to Satan, to that modern embodiment
of Satan which we know as 'radical evil'. This means that far from
calling into question the dualist tradition which locates the source
of wickedness outside what constitutes our humanity, Auschwitz
tends instead, because of its unthinkable monstrousness, to rein-
force the divide. An evil so extreme cannot have its single source in
humanity; there is something transcendent in it; it fills the place of

the absent God; it is itself a kind of negative divinity. What the Nazis
did, writes Primo Levi – Nazis like Eichmann – amounted to 'non-
human words and deeds, really counter-human'. This is why 'Perhaps one cannot, what is more one must not, understand what
happened, because to understand is almost to justify'.[25] Yet on the
next page, Levi tells us that the Nazis, Eichmann among others,
'were not born torturers, were not – with only a few exceptions –
monsters: they were ordinary men'. How can Eichmann simultaneously be the ordinary man that I am and the monster that I am
not? Levi does not ask this question, but what he wrote allows us a
glimpse of the answer which he could have given: 'Monsters exist,
but they are too few in number to be truly dangerous. More
dangerous are the common men, the functionaries ready to believe
and to act without asking questions, like Eichmann.' He concludes:
'It is, therefore, necessary to be suspicious of those who seek to
convince us with means other than reason.' All in all, in Primo
Levi's view (but probably also in the view of the majority of
enlightened minds today), the pertinent distinction is the one
between enlightenment and obscurantism: *an ordinary man at the
mercy of obscurantism becomes a monster; an ordinary but enlightened man
remains a good one.* Satan is not, then, what Milton makes of him –
in other words, the embodiment of something which is present in
all human beings. The 'foul beast' then acts upon us from outside
by contaminating us with bad ideas. This is how enlightened man
can idealize himself.

Seen in terms of Enlightenment thought, Auschwitz perpetuates
the same confusion as the story of Job. With omnipotence becoming
an essential attribute of God, and Job placing his truth in God
alone, he thereby binds his being to the enjoyment of omnipotence.
In the case of Auschwitz, the survivor is equally tempted to see in
destructive omnipotence the point of anchorage for his truth, even
if this is a transcendence of radical evil rather than a transcendence
of God. Alain Badiou is right when he says: 'Just as Lévinas
definitively suspends the originality of the opening by the Other to
the supposition of the Quite-Other [God], so the upholders of
ethics suspend consensual identification of evil on the supposition
of a *radical* Evil.'[26]

In the course of this chapter, I have tried to show that in order to think about the inner source of malice, it is necessary to emerge from monotheism and the dualism it installs, from what our secular thought preserves of these, and lastly from the idealization of self which such conceptions encourage. This is why, in Chapter 2, I pursue the inquiry by means of an experience which, while it resembles that of Job (it, too, involves an encounter with omnipotence), is, unlike his, a real – even banal – experience, whose transgressive and destructive character is not masked by any idealization. The narration of this experience will help us to get close to what constitutes the bad side of our fount of limitlessness – a bad side which leads us to confuse ourselves with a presence in the face of which nothing else can exist, thereby placing ourselves in the clutches of an absolute malice.

This story is autobiographical (it involves my first meeting with Frankenstein's creature). But it is nonetheless the account of an objective event, an experience through which, in one form or another, all children have lived.

2

The Spectre of Absolute Evil

The dining-room stove stays lit from autumn to spring. Night and day it burns, and beside it the coal scuttle stands guard, tall and narrow, like a great pitcher of blackened iron plate.

Every evening – this is one of the small tasks that falls to the children – I have to go down to the cellar to fetch coal. So every evening, after dark, I take the scuttle from the dining-room, I cross the hallway, I open the door which leads to the basement stairs. As I go down the first few steps, the feeling of cold is joined by a weight of solitude. This change of atmosphere is habitual, it is foreseeable, yet I fear it every time. After the cement-floored basement where the bikes are kept, I go through to a first cellar; the tools there, stored away tidily by my father, give the shadow a partly civilized air. One more door, then there's the coal cellar. The dim, soot-covered electric bulb is not enough to overcome the darkness. I can tell there's an earth floor, I can faintly see the wood pile and the somewhat mouldy pieces of debris coated in black dust. I bend over the heap of anthracite and start filling the scuttle. Each shovelful of coal nuts makes a clattering sound like a shower of pebbles when it hits the plate iron of the scuttle. A noise like the end of the world, which reverberates through and through to become a fiendish summons.

Then it comes – then I feel at my back the all-invading presence, the boundless threat emanating from it, the giant's bulk and the strangler's hands that move inexorably forward.

It is Frankenstein's creature.

Evening after evening, that winter when I was twelve, I am terror-stricken by a being which, nonetheless, I know very well does not exist. The dining-room, the cellar. From the one to the other and back again, always the same. Two worlds which are always just as far apart. When I go down there, it's to no avail that my parents, my brothers and my sisters are close at hand; it's to no avail that I can hear them above my head; they are of no help to me. There's nothing for it, I'm all on my own with the imaginary presence; it drowns me in its omnipotence. Having filled the scuttle in a near-frenzy, my heart hammering, I climb back up as quickly as I can, but slowed down by my burden, by the handle I have to grip in both hands.

I open the dining-room door and all trace of the monster disappears, as if it had never existed. Sometimes they look at me, taken aback by my haste. I am tight-lipped, evasive; the terror I endure cannot be confessed to. This persecution must remain secret – I don't know why.

When I think back to this long terror, I wonder why I never sought protection against the inexorable persecutor in a prayer to God. Had I straightaway given up any prospect of escape? Did it become impossible for me to find any word, any utterance to clutch at, precisely because I was confronted with an adversary alien to all society and all speech? There was no doubt in my mind then that God was all-powerful, since this was what I had been taught. But indeed, I had needed to be told so. God was omnipotent wherever some authority affirmed that he was. He was omnipotent throughout the infinite universe and through century after century, but in order to benefit from his protection one still had to be within reach of a place where this truth was inscribed and proclaimed. The omnipotence which emanated from the monster was of quite a different order: he had no need of any preacher, any doctrine, any belief. In the midst of the clatter and the darkness, his presence was affirmed by itself. I did not need to believe in it; I could feel it. It seized hold of my body and soul, horribly, and until I had resurfaced into the world of other people, I remained its prey.

Before the start of that winter, during that period when, with cold weather on the way, thoughts were turning to the need for the stove to be lit, my brother had taken me to the local cinema. They were showing a *Frankenstein* film whose title I have forgotten; but I can recall the lean face of Peter Cushing, who played the part of Victor Frankenstein, the scientist who creates the monster.

The first scene in the film which comes to mind (probably because it is not unrelated to my memory of the coal cellar) is this one. A blind old man is going through a forest, guided by a young boy. The blind man asks the child to go and fetch him some water at a nearby farm or village, and sits down on a rock to wait for him. Neither of them knows that the creature is wandering about the forest (the monster has broken the chains which confined it inside Frankenstein's manor house, and has fled). The blind man hears footsteps. He asks who it is; there is no answer. The presence of a stranger whom he can neither see nor identify. The monster snarls with rage and strangles the old man with its powerful hands.

I can also remember a corpse lying inside something resembling a large aquarium, a glass bier. A violent storm unexpectedly triggers the mechanism which is meant to bring it to life. So when Victor Frankenstein goes into his laboratory, now he finds not the bandage-swathed figure who was lying down, but a terrifying spectre which towers over him with its great bulk.

The laboratory is located in a wing of the manor house. Like Bluebeard, Victor F. has placed it out of bounds to his fiancée or his young wife, who knows nothing about his secret experiments. We see the pleasantly furnished drawing-room where the couple sometimes receive guests. Who could imagine the murky activities which the scientist pursues in the other wing of his abode, and the nightmare he is working towards?

My life resembled Victor's, split between two worlds which were impossible to unite, and I, like him, had to face alone the accursed part which I could neither share nor hold back.

In this experience, I was incomprehensible to myself. But that was not what worried me; what mattered to me more than anything was to escape the terror. All children are familiar with experiences of this kind and, like passionate lovers who desperately strive to be free of an impossible love, with the passing of time they forget in the end.

Whether it is a question of love or terror, however, once we have got through it we still have a taste for it. In the case of children, what provokes an intolerable terror in the first place usually ends up becoming bearable, in such a way that pleasure takes over from the contrasting agitation with which it continues to be mixed up. Three or four years after the *Frankenstein* which I have just mentioned, I saw another film, *The Mummy's Revenge* (or was it *Curse?*). A mummy came back to life, went to far-off England to find the archaeologists who had violated its tomb (among them the inevitable Peter Cushing), and strangled them one by one. This time things went better. I had taken the risk of returning to the source of my terror, and I had been able to enjoy it without incurring the revenge of the mummy, without finding myself implacably persecuted like the scientists who had disturbed its rest.

I shall say something at the end of this chapter about the process whereby we escape from the infinite wickedness of figures of terror, and even experience pleasure at seeing them staged as characters. Let us stay briefly with those irrational terrors of which I have given one example; how can it be that we can feel genuinely threatened by a figure whom we nonetheless know does not exist? The usual reply to this is to attribute some rational cause to fears which are not real fears; what human beings fear most is death (this commonplace, after all, is perhaps a preconception, but that does not prevent it from being received like an indisputable fact). Behind these fears without an object there might be hidden that object of fear. If we are frightened by imaginary figures such as monsters, ogres, spectres and demons, it must be because through them we are reminded of the fact that we are mortal. Once you give some thought to this explanation, it apparently explains nothing. If indeed the prospect of our own death were the true cause of the terrors which fictional beings inspire in us, these would have little effect in our early years, but increasingly more so as we approach the end of our life. Now this is precisely the reverse of what takes place: terrors of this kind are fierce in children (a child of four does not yet have an awareness of being mortal; he is no less fascinated and terrified by the wolf or the ogre). During adolescence, we are still usually fond of horror stories, but elderly people have hardly any interest in them. At the time when Frankenstein's creature terrified me, I was well aware that it was my state of being a child which made me so vulnerable to the monster, and that this boundless power of annihilation with which I was confronted spared adults – or, at any rate, did not affect them to the same extent.

It is obvious, too, that when they are convinced of their immortality, human beings are not thereby spared terrors of this kind. At the same time as it offers consolation, a belief in immortality maintains a dizzying sense of the infinite. And Christian preaching has not failed to exploit this vertigo, providing the faithful with stories depicting all the horror that the damned soul must live through beyond death for all eternity. By the sickle with which it is armed the allegory of death reminds us of our inexorable end. But it also presents a living, faceless skeleton, a being released from the limits imposed upon human beings by a definite identity. If this ageless, nameless entity takes its implacable character from the factual reality of death, it is the better to impose its spectral omnipotence. And it is this which, in reality, remains enigmatic.

There is another way of dispelling the terror effect (or other effects) which a narrative produces upon those who 'consume' it. It consists in setting aside the fact that a novel read by no one or a film seen by no one would not exist, and considering the work solely in relation to its author. Certainly, the approach which consists in studying the author and situating him or her within the historical and cultural environment is legitimate and worthwhile. It is interesting, for example, to know something about that young Englishwoman from a cultivated, nonconformist middle-class background who wrote *Frankenstein* at the age of nineteen. We might wish to know something about the ideas seething in Mary Shelley's mind: Enlightenment philosophy, revolutionary ideas, Romantic individualism, not to forget the dark repertoire freighted by the Gothic novel and a fondness for the sublime. These elements and others allow us a better reading of *Frankenstein*, helping us to grasp particular resonances and things implied within the text, and to have a better understanding of the interest it aroused in readers in the early nineteenth century.

Yet this type of exploration and interpretation has a drawback. It does in fact provide the reader, now turned commentator, with an excellent alibi for avoiding the responsibility incumbent upon him or her as reader. The reader of the story (the viewer of a film) is not in the position of someone committed to scholarship. Unlike the commentator, who can feel more detached, the reader is in some sense jointly responsible for what is staged by the narrative. It is a part of the activity of reading that the story becomes enacted, and the reader is directly repaid for this activity by the pleasure derived from it. Unlike the sleeping dream which is lived only by the maker of the dream, it is a feature of the story, because it is a daytime activity, to constitute a shared experience. Attributing a story exclusively to the author, even – or above all – when this is done through a psychoanalytic interpretation, is therefore going to result in a partially false attribution.

The difficulty of recognizing that *we have some part to play in the novel or the film which we are enjoying* is obviously attenuated by the degree to which the story brings in likeable or admirable characters; these offer us a flattering mirror. But in the case of *Frankenstein* (whether it be films or the novel), the story is so dark and violent that it suits us to attribute responsibility for it to the author, without having to linger over the idea that we too, as readers, have had a hand in it.

The story of my daily descent to the cellar shows to what extent *Frankenstein* thrust deep roots into my own heart, and not just into that of the novel's author. This is where we must begin to seek an explanation.

It is clear that I was terrified because I felt I was a prey to omnipotence – in other words, to an absolute evil. The benign infinite which feeds our ideals and our dreams is not the only form it takes; the infinity of goodness, that of the transcendent God, is not truly infinite because it guarantees coexistence (at least the coexistence of those who believe in Him). Now, by definition, real limitlessness, all-powerfulness, has no limit to be given by anyone. The radical infinite makes all forms of coexistence impossible; it is

destructive. I was terrified because, like Job, I found myself faced
with omnipotence. Not with that God who never becomes manifest
except through the mouth of those who speak in his place. More
with something like Behemoth or Leviathan, something which
exists even if no one gives it a name, a sort of primal non-being.
The expression 'accursed share' used by Georges Bataille to desig-
nate this reality is a very accurate one; so long, nevertheless, as one
does not use it, as he himself does, to valorize this reality and see in
it a 'sovereign' part. For me it is a matter, as I have said, of asking
myself questions about something rather than erecting it as a value.

The terror I suffered could have its source only in me, and that
is what I need to clarify, if only so that I do not fall back into the
rhetoric of the sublime. If, talking about my experience in the
cellar, I can say today: 'The monster is myself', I must certainly
distinguish this declaration from the valorizing identification about
which I spoke above: 'Job is myself', or: 'Christ is myself'. In this
last case, one can enjoy a strong relation to completeness – something which resembles the absolute but is not, however, the experience of a radical limitlessness: that is to say, pure and simple
destruction. This is why an identification with Job or with Christ
can give an exalting impression of attaining to an indivisible kernel
of one's own self-being. Instead, it is clear that I was incapable of
recognizing anything of myself in the monster and that, above all, I
had no wish to do so. There was nothing of the ideal in this
experience, it was not a movement towards transcendence, it had
no element of a spiritual experience. It was a part of childhood,
that is all. Besides, although the monster owed its presence to my
imagination – that is to say, to me – it was not me in the sense that
it was, far rather, the impossibility of being me, a whiff of non-being
that had spurted out of me but into which I was on the point of
disappearing, and which, for this reason, could appear only as
something outside me.

How is it possible that the monster could have derived its
existence and its power from me? Why was it necessary for me to
perceive it as a presence? And why did I feel this presence in a
dread of annihilation?

In the example I have given there is a constant which is so

widespread (we find it in all terrors of this kind) that we run the risk of paying it no attention: the opposition between two spaces, in this instance the dining-room and the cellar. On the one hand, a world where I have my place beside others, where people are clearly identified, a lighted world where things, too, are familiar and distinct. On the other, the place of the terror: an environment of darkness and solitude, subterranean like a vault. To describe the coal cellar in these terms is obviously not to give it an objective image. After all, it is only one of the rooms in the house, and the function it fulfils is quite harmless. Why not experience it in the same way as the kitchen or the living-room? Because for the child, primordial Chaos is never far away; a coal cellar is all it takes to conjure it up.

The conception of the person which is customary to us, and which matches the one bequeathed to us by Enlightenment thought, allows us little means of understanding this splitting between two spaces, nor, as a consequence, of answering the questions provoked by the spectral presence of the monster. In order to begin making these questions thinkable, we have to give up the idea that the person is constructed around a kernel (a *self*) given by nature, and that once the person is thus assured of itself, its development is equivalent to a progressive investment of its environment by knowledge and by action. Instead, we must advance the hypothesis that the true *self*, the 'authentic person', is not an inborn kernel, but that it is constituted as the child sets foot in a common world, a world where he or she is defined in relation to others, a world which enables the child gradually to assume consistency. The inborn *self*, the initial *self*, is not self, but a kind of non-bounded, non-differentiated proto-subjectivity. Thus, to answer the imperative 'Become what you are' is first to give up (inasmuch as is possible) this infinite *self* which precedes the defined *self*, just as primordial Chaos precedes the differentiated world.

'One is not born a self, one becomes one', we might say, paraphrasing Simone de Beauvoir. But we must carefully note that the celebrated formulation in *The Second Sex* ('One is not born a woman, one becomes one') is inscribed within a culturalist context: society shapes women, a shaping which constrains and represses.

My formulation – 'One is not born a self' – does not draw its meaning from this context; instead, it implies that it would be a return to our initial state which would be oppressive. In this respect, we could call upon the support of ideas forged through the experience of psychoanalysis – ideas which stress the founding character of whatever fixes or sets limits and boundaries upon the child's body and person (to quote Winnicott, Lacan, Françoise Dolto, among others). But we could equally make reference to an idea of the person which is very widespread in Africa. Contrasting with the world of the village, founded upon an order which allows people both to be distinct from one another and to coexist, there is the world of the forest and the bush – a repository of valuable energies, but also a place where predatory forces lurk. The child who is born becomes a person by taking his place among other people, in the village; but he must thereby abandon a part of himself, dissociating himself from a kind of *alter ego* which belongs in the world of the forest. Thus, being means being split: on the one hand inborn boundlessness; on the other social existence. And if this division is set up badly, if it is undermined, the person becomes the vector of forces which are made manifest in predatory form as vampirism or witchcraft.[1]

Within the context of such a conception, the fact that the cellar was not experienced as an ordinary room becomes intelligible. We can understand that the child who is alone in the dark will no longer be himself, will no longer be the same child as the one in the space of the living-room. Indeed, precisely because he is a child, he has not yet sufficiently internalized the strength to be derived from the fact of taking one's place in the world of others. His own representation of himself is not yet in a position to triumph over a sensory environment which strikes him as being apart from the world of others. Thus, inevitably, sensations of night-time solitude take him back to what he was before being himself, and he is once more bathed in the evil infinite where his being merges into nothingness and melts into limitlessness. Although the child is told repeatedly that 'there's nothing to be frightened of', there is therefore good reason why he might find himself in the grip of a dread of annihilation.

The hypothesis still needs to be filled out. In fact it does not explain why the evil infinite is experienced by the child as a *presence*. Adults, too, know boundlessness and dread, but they experience them more often in the form of depression than of terror. The depressive state can be translated into a feeling of dread of annihilation, but this feeling is not inflicted upon the adult by an omnipotent presence; what until then had been a source of relative strength is withdrawn, and he or she feels the effects of an ebbing, a low tide of being.

Children, of course, are not immune to states of depression and, in any case, they are sometimes gripped by deadly boredom. Such a state can be experienced in broad daylight, and even in the midst of other people, while terrors, as we have seen, have solitude and darkness as their specific setting. Unlike depression, terror is a state directly linked to a specific sensory environment: a picture book fixes the threatening silhouette of the wolf, pitch darkness encircles and lays siege to the body. This contains a significant clue which will help us to understand why the evil infinite is then perceived as an all-powerful presence. Light makes it possible to distinguish things and beings, just as speech makes it possible to identify them and fashion a sense of an inhabited world. Darkness, by contrast, erodes the features which allow identification; like the jaws of the wolf, it closes in on the edges of the child's body, it gives substance to the intrusion of nothingness (this is why this body has to be protected by being enveloped within the last place of safety offered by its bed, taking good care to let no hand or foot poke out). Darkness brings the child back to the dawn of himself, when the indistinctness of his soul was matched by a lack of definition about the bounds of his body. Then, the adult who took care of him was the omnipotent divinity from whom he still had little sense of being separate. Which body was the appendage, the prosthesis of the other? Certainly, the father and the mother – in theory – distinguish the child from themselves. But the baby is not yet constituted as a distinct entity. For him or her, being a self does not yet exclude being the other, and the howling helplessness of the tiny immobilized body is peculiarly combined with the strength of the giant holding it close, and at that point constituting the baby's only mirror. Insofar as it is connected to this very early experience, infinity's powerful waves threaten the integrity of both the person and his body alike. The child feels caught again by the boundless and omnipotent entity which was there before he became himself. And, as then, should there be no common world which ensures coexistence, there is no room for two, and he sees himself being inexorably annihilated by this dark divinity. This all-invading presence therefore does not correspond to any defined identity. This someone who is no one has no way of being bounded as if it were his father, or his mother, or himself; it is as much a matter of the boundlessness which he glimpses through his parents as the one which he projects upon them.[2]

The persecutor's power of destruction is the equivalent of an irresistible attraction towards crossing over or crossing out founding boundaries; the enclosure which delineates a proper name, the fragile wall of a body and a face whose form is cohesive and distinct. A necessarily predatory power, therefore: 'Only the voracity of a ferocious dog would accomplish the fury of someone bounded by nothing,' wrote Georges Bataille on the subject of Sadeian violence.[3] Frankenstein's creature needs no fangs to undo his victim's fine cohesion. His destructive power is signified by the fact that he himself has crossed out founding boundaries: he has no name. On the posters which, during Mary Shelley's lifetime, advertised theatrical adaptations of the novel, there was usually a blank space left opposite the name of the actor who embodied the monster. It was a procedure that pleased Mary Shelley: 'This nameless mode of naming the unameable', she wrote, 'is rather good.'[4] As for the creature's body, it is a nightmare vision; no other human being would be able to recognize his likeness in it.

I have shown how, in the coal cellar, my own 'evil infinite' closed in on me in the form of a destructive presence. Still to be clarified are the connections between terror and two other feelings which, although they were not in the foreground of my encounter with the monster, were no less present: guilt and desire.

Whenever I was in the living-room, I existed in the midst of my family. An existence of relationship, and therefore relative, as in all kinds of social life. Certain ways of being are appropriate with one person and inappropriate with another; certain kinds of behaviour correspond to some situations and not to others: complex limitations which are constraining and unavoidable. By internalizing them, in recompense we gain an extension of the scope of our existence in accordance with the bonds we form with those around us. But this expansion remains limited; it prohibits us from ever making an absolute and radical affirmation of ourselves. In the cellar, some form of limitless existence opened up again. I could approach it and feel all its intensity. The price to be paid, however, was also an absolute one: in its merging with me, infinity would absorb me and bring me face to face with the imminence of my own annihilation.

If transgression is the deliberate crossing of a forbidden barrier, then this was not a matter of transgression; I was not forbidden to go to the cellar, I was ordered to do so. And my encounter with the monster was not the result of a choice, since, on the contrary, its presence was imposed upon me despite all the efforts I made to exorcize it. None the less, from the point of view of what is blameworthy or legitimate, the boundary I was crossing was not insignificant; it was the frontier separating the construction of the world from its destruction (what I mean here by *world* is everything that makes possible the existence and coexistence of human beings); in other words, this was a frontier that predated all established authority. The act of crossing over which I experienced whenever I went down to the cellar was therefore a response to something which has to be called a wish, even if its fulfilment was expressed as terror and dread, and a blameworthy wish, even if the frontier crossed was not the object of any explicit prohibition.

I might have been able to understand this a few years later, when I saw the film about the mummy rising from the dead to take its revenge. I would have been able to understand it, first, because the film had offered me not only fear, but pleasure too. And because the story itself enacted the fact of entering – albeit not a cellar, but a tomb; and because this intrusion obviously answered the wish of the archaeologists. There remained, however, one notable difference between my experience and that of the men of science: in their case the punishment, which arrived quite a while after the satisfaction of their wish, was clearly distinct from it; whereas in mine, fulfilment and punishment coincided perfectly. This meant that in my confusion I could not recognize what was happening to me either as the fulfilment of a transgressive wish or as its sanction, and the experience remained as impenetrable as it was distressing.

In this respect, it was akin to the one with which Victor Franken-stein is confronted. The young scientist has only one wish – a wish beside which all else pales, even his love for his fiancée: to pierce the secret of life, to create life himself. To this end he is prepared to do anything; we see that he, too, desecrates tombs, in order to procure the flesh that he needs. And at the very point when a labour of years at last bears fruit, at the very moment when the body he has fashioned comes to life, his long-awaited fulfilment is transformed into a nightmare punishment, and he himself cannot endure the sight of what he has made. So long as the unique object of his desires was not yet a person, so long as it had not become complete, he could come near to it and work on it with his own hands. But when the thing becomes a presence, a being which casts its gaze upon him, he flees, overwhelmed with dread; in the face of radical limitlessness, one can only be annihilated.

This composite flesh to which Victor gives fresh life constitutes a new kind of ghost (this is just how Mary Shelley regarded the monster). Fear of the dead can be extended to what we have just seen regarding Victor Frankenstein. Enlightenment thought labelled the universal fear of the dead a *superstition* (the intellectual elite of the eighteenth century replaces ghosts with those bodies which are not really dead, and are given premature burial[5]). Every enlightened thinker knows that the dead do not come back to life, and no doubt it is this certainty which sometimes makes us desire the death of a person who poisons our existence. The dead do not come back to life, that is a fact; but a knowledge of this fact has never stopped anyone from believing in ghosts, nor from endowing them with a boundless malevolence; this, too, is a fact. If, contrary to 'rational' thought, we acknowledge that the radical infinite can only be a bad infinite, and that human beings have a stake in this limitlessness which is incompatible with coexistence, we can see a fear of ghosts as the manifestation of an entirely well-founded fear: *the fear of being unable to keep one's own boundlessness at a distance.*

The process of mourning is not only about the bond between oneself and the deceased person. It is just as much about the relationship one maintains with one's own boundlessness. A death which one has not mourned thus holds the same power to invade as the object of an impossible and passionate love. So many stories in the oral tradition, so many poems and novels resonate with this analogy! The author of *Frankenstein* probably knew Goethe's *The Bride of Corinth*, or Bürger's *The Ballad of Leonore* (whose subject was taken from the oral tradition, and which existed in several English translations). In both these poems, one of the lovers dies. The other does not know this (he therefore cannot mourn). When he sees the beloved, he thinks she is still alive, and she takes him with her into death. M.G. Lewis, author of the famous Gothic novel *The Monk*, spent some time at the Villa Diodati during the summer of 1816, along with Byron, Polidori and the Shelleys. He had stayed in Germany, had met Goethe, and had absorbed folklore and ballads like Bürger's. He liked telling ghost stories. This one in particular: a young man is called to his regiment; his wife waits for him inconsolably. One evening she hears him coming back, but when she sees the fatal wound on his brow, she realizes that she is dealing with a ghost. He manages to reassure her. However, one night when, engrossed in the pleasures of a ball, she fails to hear the bell which regularly announces the phantom's coming, it drags her away to her death.[6] When the beloved and benevolent being becomes truly boundless, it mutates into a pure force of annihilation.

During their stay on the shores of Lake Geneva, Shelley, Byron, and the young Mary also read a collection of ghost stories, which had been translated from German into French. As every introduction to *Frankenstein* points out, these spine-chilling tales made them want to invent their own. After a conversation about galvanism and the spark of life, Mary was haunted into the small hours by nightmare images. This nightmare supplied her with the core of her novel: 'What terrified me will terrify others,' she thought.[7]

One of the tales of horror that Mary had read told the story of a woman who is deserted by her husband and dies in solitude. She presents herself to the man as if she were still alive, then takes her revenge on him, revealing her spectral nature (this is probably a universal plot theme; at any rate, it is also to be found in the collection of Japanese tales compiled by Lafcadio Hearn[8]).

The story resembles that of *Ondine*, a poetic narrative which La Motte-Fouqué, a German Romantic, had published in 1811. Ondine, a water sprite, returns to the man who has loved her; she returns on the very evening when he has just married another woman, and drags her former husband to his death. Two themes are combined: non-mourning (in reality the man still loves Ondine) and revenge (the forsaken wife takes back her husband for ever). There is the same boundless grief which circulates between the man who remains and the woman who has been rejected, and the return of the dead woman answers both of their desires. But at the same time this return constitutes a punishment, a punishment which the husband draws down upon himself because he has forgotten his first wife and because it is impossible for him to mourn her.

This paradox has its own logic, one which is applicable to relationships between the living and the dead not only in fiction, but also in reality. The living, as we have seen, have reason to fear the dead whenever they are unable to separate from them, and they use them to fill their own boundlessness. But forgetting someone who has died, obliterating the bond one has had with him or her when alive, is no better. It is a way of shunning that frontier of the self which constituted that bond; instead of granting the dead person a place without limits, one is abolishing the place altogether, which is still a way of bypassing boundaries – those founding boundaries which guarantee to each of us a *place of being*.

In this respect, the relationships between the living and the dead constitute only one particular instance of the relationships between human beings. In the most general terms it could be formulated thus: *there can be no viable relationship between two beings if one of them occupies a non-place*. Non-place can be taken as meaning *nothing*: the infinity of the one reduces the place of the other to nothing. Or *everything*: the one invades the infinity of the other.

This chapter has enabled us to uncover a specific form of the fantasy of omnipotence: the fantasy of a being which is totally wicked. In order to conclude, I still have to show how the shift from fantasy to reality comes about.

Popular tales, novels, fantasy and action films give substance to this fantasy by clothing it in images fashioned from the visible world. They confer on it a *semblance* of reality. From this point of view, Frankenstein's creature is only one figure among others in the vast gallery of spectres of absolute evil: ogres, wolves, witches, devils, vampires and mad scientists bent on destroying the world in order to dominate it, serial killers and other master-criminals. In the James Bond films, for example, we can easily see how the 'arch-villain' simultaneously presents some of the unreal features of fantasy (such as the shadowy boss of the criminal organization known as 'Spectre') and borrows others from reality (spying, technology, the Cold War, etc.). Films of this kind help us to understand what a fine and porous line separates fiction from reality.

Here, we can take reality to mean two things: on the one hand, the real behaviour of a person or a group of people (for example, the behaviour of this or that American Indian or tribe of Indians in a particular period); on the other, the beliefs and convictions concerning this person or group. These beliefs can be false, they can resemble fictions, but for those who subscribe to them they are quite real. Here, for example, is what one chief administrator for Indian affairs wrote in the mid-nineteenth century:

> Which of us has not listened with sensations of horror to nursery stories that are told of the Indian and his cruelties? In an infant mind he stood for the Moloch of our country. We have been made to hear his yell; and to our eyes have been presented his tall, gaunt form with the skins of beasts dangling around his limbs, and his eyes like fire, eager to find some new victim on which to fasten himself, and glut his appetite for blood.[9]

The author admits that this image of the Indian derives in part from fiction (from stories for children), but that does not prevent him from believing that it contains a good deal of truth; fantasy and fiction feed into the ways in which the author and other American colonists picture the Indians. The malevolence attributed to them therefore has two sources. One is the quite real cruelty demonstrated by a certain number of Indian warriors, rightly feared by those who had come to appropriate their land. The other source is the fantasy of absolute evil which these same colonists projected on to the Indians. As Michael Rogin accurately observes: 'Indian atrocities . . . not only justified war against Indians; in response to Indian violence whites themselves engaged in fantasies and activities expressing primitive rage.'[10] This, therefore, is not just a matter of turning the other into the aggressor in order to present one's own aggression as self-defence. It is also about the exhilarating sense of attaining a superior finality, which derives from *the felt need to compete with the limitlessness which has been projected on to the other.*

This sequence can be generalized in the following terms: I perceive myself as 'good' (even if some of my actions as seen by others are not deemed 'good'); I am conscious that someone with whom I have dealings is carrying out an act of aggression towards me; I project my fantasy of all-powerfulness (of all-malignity) on to him; since the other is all, I am going to be annihilated; to defend myself against this annihilation, I myself must be all – a whole, undivided, total being. Thus I shall abandon myself to the pleasure of all-powerfulness (while continuing to believe that I am good, and that it is the other who is malign). Through this sequence we can see how it is possible to reach a transgressive finality (while at the same time believing it to be legitimate) from the point when, instead of identifying directly with the bad infinite of total malignity, one identifies with it through an interposed mirror (for example, by seeing oneself as someone confronted with a diabolical plot – a plot hatched by the CIA, the Jews, the Communists, foreigners in general, extraterrestrials, etc.).

Action films supply countless examples of this mimetic sequence, with the result that the spectator is happy to participate in the omnipotence demonstrated by a hero who stands alone against everyone else (Rambo, for example) – an omnipotence which, however, is no different from the kind that overwhelms and frightens him when it is demonstrated by a demoniacal character who is boundlessly malign. If the mechanisms of malignity in fiction are the same as those in reality, should we thereby consider that the pleasure experienced by the audience is bad, and that they are corrupted by the violence of the cinema? There is no simple answer to this question. Indeed, on the one hand, as is repeatedly stressed, young audiences can be fascinated by fictional characters who exercise violence and, as a result, wish to be like them. On the other hand, the very fact that these characters appear in fiction – that is to say, in the realm of play and pretence – makes an essential contribution to the process whereby we can establish a certain distance between our fount of limitlessness and ourselves. The spectacle of a mummy rising from the dead to strangle the scientists who have desecrated its tomb one by one, and the spectacle of Rambo's killing spree, do not introduce into the mind of the spectator a malice which was not there before; they reveal it, which is quite different (likewise, the image of a sexual object does not introduce a desire from which we would otherwise have been preserved; it reveals the presence of this desire in us). In the face of the threat inherent within this revelation, there are three possible attitudes:

- because of a failure to distinguish between the level of fiction and that of reality, we see in it an encouragement to exercise in earnest the violence of the omnipotent character;
- instead, we cast this violence outside us; such a rejection entails two consequences: first, the bad infinite which is within us remains strange and unknown, therefore just as virulent; in the second place, this repression deprives us simultaneously of the good side of our limitlessness, of the energy and joy whose source it is;
- lastly, we face up to the pleasure afforded us by the spectacle of violence, we acknowledge that a part of our energy is stimulated by bad feelings, we recognize that evil does us good. And in fact, from the point when we take on total-wickedness in a space of play – from the point when, as a result, we appropriate it *as a pretence* (as children do in the game of 'bogey man', or when they act out other figures of omnipotence) – evil does us good. We

identify more in earnest (that is to say, unknowingly) with our fount of limitlessness, we continue to be connected to it, but with a distance and disidentification which introduce an awareness that fiction and play are not reality.[11]

There is something paradoxical in the idea that a genuine psychic vitality can depend upon pretence. Authors such as Nietzsche or Bataille have been somewhat uncomfortable with it (they are by no means the only ones), and it is one of Lacan's great virtues that he, on the contrary, upheld and developed this idea. If one allows, as I tried it to show in Chapter 1, that goodness and being do not arise from a *single* source, but from a compromise or a marriage which comes about between two sources, this idea ceases to be paradoxical; inasmuch as pretence, representation, takes as its source our fundamental limitlessness, the vital link with it is maintained; and inasmuch as we make do with its representation (and therefore with a reality which is simultaneously bounded and meaningful for others), we maintain simultaneously a link which is no less vital, that of coexistence with others. In this sense, the reading of a work about malignity can turn out not to be depressing, as one might fear, but invigorating.

We shall see in Chapter 3 that the important thing about Victor Frankenstein, the scientist who creates the monster, is precisely that he refuses to make do with a pretence of limitlessness.

3

Victor Frankenstein's Excess

In films, interest focuses most of all on the monster; while the novel centres on the infernal partnership formed by the creator and his creature. I was about thirty when I read *Frankenstein*. The pleasure I derived from reading it was not, strictly speaking, the pleasure of fear; it was more that of finding in it a charm which was no doubt antiquated, but unexpected – unexpected because the different versions popularized by the cinema have, as a whole, set aside the most romantic aspects of the story. So I discovered that the character of the creature was far from being that of a mere scarecrow emitting inarticulate grunts. It was a being capable of expressing itself in long tirades worthy of a character out of Shakespeare or Milton; able to read (Milton's *Paradise Lost*, to be precise, Goethe's *Werther*, and even Plutarch). It was also a being which was interested in others, and felt the most human emotions. I discovered the idyllic families formed by the subsidiary characters (Mary Shelley had read Rousseau's *La Nouvelle Héloïse*) – but also, in contrast to these harmonious tableaus, wild and desolate places in the midst of which the most violent feelings erupted. A glacier beneath the towering Mont Blanc, a far-flung island off the coast of Scotland, polar wastes (partly inspired by Coleridge's *The Rime of the Ancient Mariner*) where Victor and his creature will finally meet their death.

These two characters bound passionately together seemed to me to exemplify the converse of the idyll: they were the negative of *Paul et Virginie*. I had a sense that the novel was unearthing unpleasant truths. It spoke to me of my youthful love affairs; it pitilessly magnified their bad sides.

At the time when I first read *Frankenstein*, I settled for the impression that it was a long family row, and made no effort to find out anything more about it. Today, rereading *Frankenstein*, I see a confirmation of my first impression. This time, therefore, I shall have to define it, and work out what led up to that feeling. But before reaching that point, we first have to get to know Victor Frankenstein more thoroughly.

Let us start by bringing to mind an interpretation of Mary Shelley's novel which is both prevalent and obvious: that *Frankenstein* illustrates the theme of the sorcerer's apprentice: of the scientist who gets carried away by science's powers, only to see the disastrous consequences of going too far rebound upon himself and on others. This way of summarizing the plot is not mistaken, but it leaves out what is best, most intense and specifically nasty about the story.

It is true that Victor obstinately pursues his project, losing sight of everything that should divert him from it. In this respect, he seems to prefigure that type of character which the adventure story has exploited unceasingly, from Jules Verne to Ian Fleming: the megalomaniac scientist whom the cinema has so often shown us reigning over his secret laboratory (set up preferably in the underground regions of a volcanic island), and engaged in an enterprise as destructive as it is titanic.

The goal pursued by Victor can even remind us of current achievements in biology, like *in vitro* fertilization or cloning. Yet the desire which animates the biologists who undertake this kind of experimentation is not necessarily of the same order as the desire which the character of Victor embodies; the fact that a fantasy scenario and a real action resemble one another does not prove that the real action is of the same transgressive and pernicious variety as the fantasy. Thus, the first doctors to cut open corpses for dissection were not necessarily enacting a fantasy of necrophilia and violating the integrity of the human body.

Certainly, it is always possible to read within the explicit themes of a narrative a lesson about factual reality. Thus, just as *Little Red Riding Hood* would speak to children about the danger of talking to strangers, *Frankenstein* warns us against extravagant scientific ambitions. But even when it corresponds to the intentions declared by the story's author, this kind of interpretation delivers only a superficial account of how narratives truly live – in other words, the action which they exert upon us. Whether it be a tale, a novel or a film, we should not confuse the manifest content of the story's events with *how it makes its mark on us*. The theme of the scientist's quest for scientific and technical domination relates to the manifest content. The effect which reading *Frankenstein* has had on me and on generations of readers certainly cannot be reduced to the mere scope of a fable.

Let us try to draw out the features which define the desire embodied in the character of Victor. 'Life and death', he says, 'appeared to me ideal bounds, which I should first break through.' For him, giving birth or bringing what is dead back to life is one and the same thing. This is why Victor is 'forced to spend days and nights in vaults and charnel-houses', and has to pursue his ghastly work in secret, as he 'dabbled among the unhallowed damps of the grave or tortured the living animal to animate the lifeless clay'. He reflects that eventually: 'A new species would bless me as its creator.' The desire to transgress the boundary separating the living from the dead is implicitly but inevitably associated with a challenge to sexual difference. 'After days and nights of incredible labour and fatigue, I succeeded in discovering the cause of generation and life'.[1] Knowing how babies are made is nothing in comparison to such a secret: what interests Victor is obviously not making a baby with his fiancée, Elisabeth; it is making one by himself.

Victor, it seems, wants to take the place of God, or of that Prometheus who gave form to the first man. Yet not exactly. Because both God and Prometheus take it for granted that to create a human being is to produce a being who is different from themselves; that endowing this being with a self-consciousness necessitates giving him a place, a site of being that is distinct from the one occupied by themselves. Whereas what drives Victor to create a being is precisely a desire in opposition to the order of the world, in opposition to the distinction of sites of being: *a desire which abolishes all limits, and thereby all possible room for the new being.*

The novel carefully retraces the genesis of this desire. Like all desires, it is rooted in infinity. But the distinctive characteristic of Victor's desire is the refusal to leave infinity behind, the refusal to engage in a process which would lead him to come to terms with a world whose order implies differences and founding boundaries. Having always been 'imbued with a fervent longing to penetrate the secrets of nature', young Victor is enthused by the alchemists of old and the search for the elixir of life. When he is about fifteen, however, the spectacle of a violent storm gives a new turn to his passion:

> As I stood at the door, on a sudden I beheld a stream of fire issue from an old and beautiful oak, which stood about twenty yards from our house; and so soon as the dazzling light vanished, the oak had disappeared, and nothing remained but a blasted stump. When we visited it the next morning, we found the tree shattered in a singular manner. It was not splintered by the shock, but entirely reduced to thin ribbons of wood. I never beheld anything so utterly destroyed.

This idea of destruction reappears a good many times in the course of the story. Two pages further on, Victor states: 'Destiny . . . had decreed my utter and terrible destruction.' Speaking of his meeting with a scientist who will play a vital role in his studies, he says: 'Chance – or rather the evil influence, the Angel of Destruction'; and what the professor says is intended for Victor's 'destruction'. Thus wickedness does not appear as an act of free will, or of a will blinded by ignorance. Here it is the result of the impossibility of existing within certain limits. It is therefore not only turned upon others, it equally exerts its effects upon Victor himself.

Lightning is omnipotence in action. In an instant, lightning crosses that expanse which separates heaven from earth. It short-circuits the zone which usually keeps each of the two orders of reality at a distance from one another – rather as the lava which gushes out of a volcano violently unites the subterranean world with the surface of the earth. Thus, fiercely, it spills out the infinite upon the finite. At the University of Ingolstadt, Victor learns to forsake Albertus Magnus and Paracelsus for modern science – as he says himself: 'to exchange chimeras of boundless grandeur for realities of little worth'. Exchanging chimeras for realities, yes. But renouncing the infinite for mediocrity, no. Victor will therefore use modern sciences, but in order to penetrate those very secrets of 'immortality and power' which the alchemists pursued.

In James Whale's film (1931), it is by using a kite to capture the electricity of storm clouds that Victor gives life to his creature. The screenwriter's inspiration for this device, which is not in the novel, was a biography by Thomas Jefferson Hogg, a friend of Percy Bysshe Shelley, in which he recalls conversations he had with the young poet. In his Promethean zeal to uncover divine fire, Shelley was working on the idea of 'electrical kites' that could 'draw down lightning from the sky'. 'What a terrible organ would the supernal shock prove, if we were able to guide it; how many of the secrets of nature would such a stupendous shock unlock!'[2] By taking his inspiration from the poet, the screenwriter did in fact remain faithful to the character of Victor as Mary Shelley had imagined him. In fact, many features of Victor were inspired by her husband – including a certain destructive bent in which her own adolescence probably inclined her to participate, but which must also have caused her anxiety, especially when one of those close to her was touched by death. And there was quite a hecatomb around her; at the time when she wrote *Frankenstein*, and was still only Shelley's mistress, there was the suicide of her half-sister, then of the poet's first wife, who was pregnant. Her own mother had died a few days after giving birth to her, and she herself was to lose three of her children. Finally, Shelley was drowned (he had set sail in weather conditions so unfavourable that it seemed likely the boat would go down). 'It seems as if the destruction that is consuming me were as an atmosphere which wrapt & infected everything connected with me,'[3] Shelley wrote in a letter to a friend in 1820.

What can one say about a desire to create life which merges with a desire for omnipotence and destruction? It is *a desire for self-begetting in completeness.* This answer will seem clearer once we have approached the character of Victor from a different angle.

Victor is not only fascinated by omnipotence; he is equally consumed, as we have seen, by the desire to pierce the secret of life. Readers or viewers of *Frankenstein* will have no difficulty in connecting with this kind of curiosity; which child has not been fascinated by the mysteries of sexuality and procreation? In each one of us a fantasy has been forged by a burning curiosity about this secret: what was then beyond our reach urged itself upon us as the place of a boundless enjoyment, arousing in us a febrile, tortured lust. In it was what parents reserved for themselves, and was forbidden to us. And beyond this reality, or at the heart of it, there was the infinite bliss which alone could fulfil our desire, there was the total origin which alone could offer our being a fitting foundation. What was imagined about our parents' real intimacy already contained something troubling. But, carried towards the abyss of a superlative pleasure, our imagination did not stop there. Indeed, the obscure sense of our infinity could not without difficulty adapt itself to the limitations implied by sexual reproduction: how, in our awareness of being one, could we have issued from two beings, not one singly? How was it possible that we could be the fruit of a contingent coming together of two ordinary people? How could we accept that we in no way presided at this event but that, on the contrary, it was carried out without us, in a world unknown to us?

I would say (for once making use of psychoanalytic language) that fantasies of the primal scene – precisely because they are fantasies, not just memories linked to the sexual relations of parents – in their archaic forms join up with those narcissistic fantasies in which the image of the self invades everything, to the point of overwhelming the very self which identifies with this all-beingness.

Victor – this is one of the reasons why *Frankenstein* has become a myth – makes the wish we all have come true. Refusing to recognize himself in the reductive mirror held up to him by the reality of familial bonds, he dedicates himself to his own regeneration, to the rebegetting of himself through the appropriation of the source of life and the reaching of the place where his own completeness is located. He dedicates himself to a calvary, that of creating by himself the Eucharist which will concentrate the infinity of his being – a blasphemous Eucharist, for it is not the bread representing the redemptive sacrifice, it is the very flesh of the sacrifice.

This explains why his creature is not baptized with any name of its own. How could its creator give it a name, since he is neither its father nor its mother? And how could the creature enjoy the status of the human person, since it is only the completion sought by Victor in answer to his desire for himself; since it is the object of which he expects the impossible: that it fill the void of his own infinity?

The creature does indeed have something of the limitless, the monstrous, the omnipotent about it. If, however, it embodies Victor's bad infinite, it can offer no remedy; at the very moment when Victor's desire reaches its goal, at the moment when 'the thing' opens its eyes for the first time, its creator makes the terror-stricken discovery that his creature is *someone other* than himself. A limitless other, in which as a consequence, at the moment when he sees the ending of his quest, he simultaneously sees his own destruction.

When I described my encounters with the monster in the coal cellar, I talked about transgression and punishment; I talked about the terror which I bore alone like a guilty secret; in this I was akin to Victor, who would talk about his solitary labours in these terms: 'I shunned my fellow-creatures as if I had been guilty of a crime.' Transgression consists in rejecting otherness – rejecting it because the dream of being oneself requires, ultimately, that one be all, and consequently that no others should exist. Punishment, in its most frightening form, is the effect of a necessary and imminent reversal, that of the dream changing into a nightmare. Since in fact every individual has no site of being except to occupy a place that is named and bounded, his or her dream of limitlessness turns back on itself into a nightmare of annihilation. This is what Mary Shelley stresses in the plainest possible way in the key episode when the creature comes to life. 'now that I had finished, the beauty of the dream vanished, and breathless horror and disgust filled my heart'.

Victor rushes out of his laboratory and takes refuge in his bedroom, where he eventually sinks into a fitful sleep. He then has a dream which, in fact, turns into a nightmare: at first Victor embraces his lovely fiancée, Elisabeth: 'but as I imprinted the first kiss on her lips, they became livid with the hue of death; her features appeared to change, and I thought that I held the corpse of my dead mother in my arms; a shroud enveloped her form, and I saw the grave-worms crawling in the folds of flannel'. In the dream of love, there are still two individuals. Incest, necrophilia – that is total union, a union that nothing limits! Victor wakes up and, in the gloom, catches sight of the monster watching him with its glassy eyes, the 'demoniacal corpse', which stretches out its fleshless hand as if to clutch him.

In all his creative exaltation, Victor does not know, nor does he wish to know, that his excessive compulsion makes him a wicked man. If someone had attempted to warn him against the implications of his unprecedented project, he would probably have brushed their criticism aside. He could have done so with an answer similar to the one which Goebbels addressed in April 1933 to the orchestra conductor Wilhelm Furtwängler, in reply to the reservations the latter had expressed about his actions:

> Politics too is an art, perhaps even the highest and broadest art in existence, and we who are giving form to modern German politics feel ourselves to be like artists to whom has been entrusted the great responsibility of shaping the rough-hewn masses into the full and solid image of the *Volk*. The mission of art and the artist is not just to unite, it goes much further. It is their duty to create, to give form, to eliminate what is sick and open the way to what is healthy.[4]

Creating out of the 'rough-hewn masses'. Creating the new man, and the unity of an organic society, was also the mission which Lenin claimed for himself. For him it was a matter of raising the masses 'into a historic creative work' on the model of the 'great mechanical industry, which rightly forms the source and basis of socialism'. This 'demands a unity of will. . . . How can a rigorous unity of will be guaranteed? By submitting the will of thousands of people to the will of one alone.'[5]

Even a lowly manager in business or the civil service is tempted to justify in his own eyes his will to act because of circumstances and the necessity to remedy them, the benefits of change, and the whole weight of opposition to this. From here it is an easy step to radicalize this as an evil and idealize the objective he has in mind and, above all, to acknowledge its necessity. Moved to act, he becomes ever blinder to the unconscious desire which motivates him, and fails to see that behind the greatness of his task, behind the determination of his will, in reality there lurks his own fount of limitlessness. This is how economic rationality and the fury to go ever further feed on one another.

4

The Infernal Couple

In 1816, the very year when Mary began writing *Frankenstein*, Benjamin Constant published *Adolphe*, a story inspired by his relationship with Madame de Staël, in which, with cruel lucidity, he testifies to the impossibility of living out limitlessness as a couple. Victor Frankenstein and his creature also testify to this impossibility, doomed as they are to a fate to which each one of us comes close, fears, avoids and, sometimes, meets: the fate of those loves where, unknowingly and with the best intentions, *each asks the other both to fill his or her infinity and for deliverance from it*, with the result that the lovers, together with their fine ideal and their dignity, sink into the dark waters of confusion and malignity.

Victor and the monster will confront one another in a grandiose domestic row, and the setting for this is on a par with their passions.[1] Ever since what had been for both of them a kind of primal scene, time has passed. The creature has led a solitary life, wandering around as an outcast. In revenge for having been rejected, it has strangled Victor's young brother and let an innocent woman be condemned in its place. For his part, in flight from the guilt and despair which gripped him, Victor embarks on a long walk in the Chamonix Valley, a landscape dear to him from childhood. This picture has as its keynote the *sublime*, a word which repeatedly issues from Mary Shelley's pen (one gets a strong sense in this passage that the author shares the tastes of her husband, who devoted a poem in the same vein to Mont Blanc).

'The immense mountains and precipices that overhung me on every side – the sound of the river raging among the rocks, and the dashing of the waterfalls around, spoke of a power mighty as Omnipotence. . . .' 'Immense glaciers approached the road; I heard the rumbling thunder of the falling avalanche and marked the smoke of its passage. Mont Blanc, the supreme and magnificent Mont Blanc, raised itself from the surrounding *aiguilles*, and its tremendous *dome* overlooked the valley.' Victor relishes his solitude in this 'terrifically desolate' setting: 'the presence of another would destroy the solitary grandeur of the scene'. The description seems like an echo from the pages of Kant. In fact, in developing his concept of the sublime, Kant had liked to imagine a being who was benevolent towards men but disappointed by them, and would take pleasure in his own isolation from the whole of society; he had pictured the traveller crossing the Alps, feeling conquered by what, in the *Critique of Judgement*, he calls 'an interesting sadness', and being elevated by sublimity above any palpable concerns.

But Victor is wrenched away from contemplation. The other looms into sight, the solitary, wandering other, his monstrous reflection! Then the nameless creature throws all the weight of its anguish and distress upon him, the one who had hoped to uplift his soul in tranquillity. This weight, which will crush Victor right to the end of the novel, is presented to him by the monster as a debt: 'Do your duty towards me, and I will do mine towards you.' With these words, the monster seems to situate its relationship with Victor within the framework of a contract. But the bond that unites them is everything but a contract: it is dark, it is indissoluble, and it involves them to the very core. Moreover, the monster reminds Victor of this: 'you, my creator, detest and spurn me, thy creature, to whom thou art bound by ties only dissoluble by the annihilation of one of us'. Bonds that are indissoluble and, what is more, unnameable; the two characters, as we have seen, do not occupy in relation to one another any defined place, any place marked out by rights and duties that refer to the order of social life. Certainly, one is the creator and the other his creature. However, while these two words imply an absolute stake, they assume no meaning either in the order of relations of kinship, or in that of an order willed by God.

This is when we should recall that Mary Shelley had dedicated *Frankenstein* to her father; but that she had also set as an epigraph these lines from Milton:

> Did I request thee, Maker, from my clay
> To mould me Man? Did I solicit thee
> From darkness to promote me?[2]

Thus, Mary was drawing a parallel between Frankenstein's creature and Adam cursing his condition after the fall – while discreetly drawing her father's attention to her own problems with life (rather like those adolescents who, in a nihilistic phase, say they didn't ask to be born; a reproach, a cry for help, but also a hate-filled rage at not being able to be at one's own origin, at not being able to be one's self by oneself).

Victor is caught in the trap of a relationship which, born of his own limitlessness, extends beyond him; he is chained by a bond which can neither be broken nor controlled; he is crushed by a debt of which he can neither be rid nor acquit himself. His reactions will therefore be those of impotence. An obstacle which prevents us from existing and against which we can do nothing impels us to affirm ourselves *regardless*. A raw, regressive affirmation full of rage, fuelled by elemental fantasies of impotence, and one which thereby comes close to the tyrant's excess. The tyrant is wicked because he can see no limits to his power. The powerless man is wicked out of revolt against his powerlessness.

The most violent of Victor's impotent reactions is the expression of a wish for the monster's death. Victor can be compared to those parents who perceive their lives as being poisoned by the child's coming into the world. Thus (as related to me by a London friend), in the hospital where ill-treated infants are cared for, when the parents come to visit; they are left alone with the child, but with a camera secretly recording their behaviour. Some of them pinch the baby, twist his arm and tell him: 'You came into the world just to piss us off!'

The desire for death can explode in the domestic quarrel, too. In order to kill his strange consort, Victor will pursue it as far as the polar wastes, but to no avail: this 'fiend', as he calls it, is indestructible. In the case of a real couple, it is certainly possible to kill one's partner, but this comes down to swapping one millstone for another: turning into a murderer and remaining one until the end of one's days. How can one get rid of the other without killing him? By fleeing from him? Victor flees. He strives to forget, he makes a pretence to others, he acts as if everything were normal. Like Stevenson's Doctor Jekyll or Perrault's Bluebeard, he leads a double life. Like them, he presents himself as outwardly pleasant, and keeps secret the passion that grips him. But each of the murders committed by the creature weighs Victor down more heavily with the burden of what cannot be confessed. Hide, hide at any price; cultivate the illusion of a regained footing in normal life; bury the overpowering transgression deep within oneself. In the quarrel more than in love, one loses restraint and dignity; for the appetite for the worst goes further than the appetite for the best. But the day after, the horrible words one has blurted out are the object of a real amnesia. Guilt and shame lead one to close thick doors on this chaos, and seek refuge in the appearances of normality.

But the other pursues Victor with its condemnation. The creature's affirmation of its persecutory omnipotence is a response to its creator's excess. A stake of being and nothingness on a world scale: for Victor, there is nowhere left. In the domestic quarrel, the one running away slams the door when he leaves, or he packs a suitcase, or lingers in a café in the hope of avoiding a predictable confrontation. But his flight is to no avail; the storm that must break will break, and the breath of air snatched here or there will have brought only a brief respite. I don't know whether the relationship between Shelley and Mary was a stormy one, but what the young woman would have known about the relationship between Byron and his wife was in any case sufficient inspiration. When Mary met him in Switzerland during the famous summer of 1816, Byron was, like Victor, a kind of criminal on the run; the hatred with which his wife pursued him and her knowledge of his incestuous secret made her someone to be feared.[3]

The confrontation with this other in whom is embodied his bad infinite whips up Victor's hatred. He explodes into insults and curses which echo far into the distance of the snows and crevasses. And then, when the monster's distress shows through its fury, and the merciless battle has a brief respite, Victor lets himself be won over by compassion, perhaps in the belief that some kind of appeasement is possible. The monster will make the most of this openness to tell Victor about its life as a wandering orphan. In a row, too, when, after violence has been unleashed, the two protagonists find that they are worn out, they fall back on hoping that the miracle of some re-found sweetness will come to save them from hell.

The monster, for its part, is condemned to a no lesser impotence than Victor's. But in it this impotence is displayed so overwhelmingly that it seeks, by a paradoxical reversal, to turn it into a source of power over Victor. In the domestic row, this desire for reversal can be expressed thus: 'Look at what a state I'm in because of you! See what you're doing to me!'

This fundamental posture on the part of the monster is, first and foremost, an accusation. If I am a victim – a total victim – all the monstrousness which apparently characterizes me in fact rebounds upon the other, the tormentor. The hatred Victor feels for his offspring can never bring him any real relief, for he cannot forget that through it is expressed the horror inspired in him by the enterprise which he himself undertook, whereas the hatred felt by the monster is experienced as justified ('I am filled with hate,' it might say). And what a pleasure it is to hate when the hatred is fed by a legitimate accusation! In the upheaval of the domestic row, of separation or divorce, each member of the couple is tempted to allow themselves this compensation. Obviously it is not a matter of making the other see that he or she is hated more than he or she hates us. It is a matter of making him or her recognize how much he or she is in the wrong, of giving oneself the advantage over him or her and the full enjoyment of legitimate hatred.

For the monster, the aggressive display of its distress also constitutes a demand. As is often the case in a row, the demand underlying an expression of distress weighs intolerably upon the other. It is not in fact a demand for something within limits – a demand to which, consequently, it would be possible to agree – but a demand which is in essence ontological. The distress involved in fact greatly exceeds the demand through which it is manifest; it is the distress of a feeling of nonexistence. One drowns in one's own limitlessness – the terror, but also the fascination felt by someone to whom there remains, as for Coleridge's *Ancient Mariner* lost in the polar wastes, only an awareness of being surrounded by a boundless void. The child turns to the adult, the lover to the beloved, and, attributing to them a superior power, makes them the object of an agonized prayer: 'You can't leave me like this!' Or, having found no recourse in human authorities, the one bereft of being turns to a Father or Mother with the status of divinities: '*De profundis clamavi ad te, Domine!*' Mary Shelley wanted the monster to be a bearer, like Job or Adam after the fall, of that incomprehensible and unjustifiable grief which threatens all consciousness of the self.

And indeed, it is only God who could respond to such a demand, for it goes beyond what one human being has the power to do for any other. For the person who makes it, however, the demand appears reasonable; it asks only for what would be normal. 'It's not exactly a lot to ask!' Yes, for one of the two, it is a vital minimum. But for the other, it's too much. So the latter is left paralysed, mute, and in the eyes of the one who feels as if he is losing his footing, he or she seems like someone who stands on the edge of the cliff, cruel and indifferent, refusing to stretch out a hand.

What the monster asks of Victor, after telling the story of its solitary life, is that he create a female companion for it – that he treat it like Adam, not like Satan, the fallen angel, cast out for ever. 'What I ask of you is reasonable,' it says. But for Victor, to agree to such a demand would be to plunge even deeper still into a destructive transgression whose burden is already intolerable to him; the accursed couple would reproduce, and it 'might make the very existence of the species of man a condition precarious and full of terror'. This is why, having set to work, Victor destroys the half-finished creature and throws the gruesome remains into the sea, thereby exposing himself to a perpetual vendetta on the part of the monster, whom he sentences to never-ending solitude. (The novel's plot differs, as we can see, from the one popularized by the cinema; in *The Bride of Frankenstein*, Victor makes a female creature, but at the sight of the monster she is horrified and rejects it.) In the passage concerning the monster's possible posterity, Mary Shelley recalls the lines in *Paradise Lost* where Adam sees the curse of original sin being extended to his descendants:

> All that I eat or drink, or shall beget,
> Is propagated curse. O voice, once heard
> Delightfully, 'Increase and multiply;'
> Now death to hear! For what can I increase
> Or multiply, but curses on my head?
> Who of all ages to succeed, but feeling
> The evil on him brought by me, will curse
> My head? 'Ill fare our ancestor impure;
> For this we may thank Adam;' but his thanks
> Shall be the execration . . .[4]

In the mind of Mary Shelley, Victor's intemperance and its effects are not without an analogy in the theology of the first transgression and fall. Only, in the novel, the role of Adam eating from the tree of knowledge is played by Victor, while the monster born of this transgression embodies Adam after the fall. From the infinite as a conquest is born the infinite as a defeat. From the power to attain limitlessness is born the curse of a sense of nonexistence.

The subjective posture which the monster depicts – 'See what you're doing to me!' – does not just constitute an accusation and an agonized prayer. It is also a threat. The excess of its grief compels the monster to invest its devastating energy in actions designed to procure some form of reparation for it, and to overturn its crushing dependence on Victor. When *Frankenstein* appeared, *The Quarterly Review* published an article by a critic in which the following remark stands out: the monster has 'the good sense to detest his creator for imposing upon him such a horrible burden as conscious existence'.[5] Yes, Victor has given it a consciousness of self, but he has not given it what would lighten its weight: a defined and legitimate place in the world of others. Nor has he given it what would fill this void: the enjoyment of a positive and full infinity.

As a result, the rage which animates the monster presents two aspects, two components which need to be distinguished all the more since, both in life and in this character, they mingle and become confused. The first aspect corresponds to a legitimate complaint: *It is unjust that another should have the power to deprive me of myself.* The second is the reflection, the response to the intemperance which characterizes Victor and of which the monster is the consequence: *I refuse to go through another in order to be myself.*

If I can neither obtain my own sense of existing from the other nor attain it without him, then, condemned to the non-being of infinity, I shall draw from it the destructive omnipotence that it contains, and I shall unleash it on the other, even if it should annihilate me too! Thus I shall extract from my own depths the power to invade the soul of the other, and to reign there. Thus I shall obtain, despite him, the pleasure of which he stands in the way: the pleasure of inverting nothing into everything.

The monster will therefore kill those who are close to Victor one by one. And in conclusion, since the latter refuses to create a female companion for it, it will strangle his young wife on the very night of their wedding. The monster thereby makes itself the master of its master. However, as it confesses at the end of the novel: 'I was the slave, not the master, of an impulse, which I detested, yet could not disobey.' Thus, it is in the impulse of its bad infinity that the monster finds its fulfilment, until, like some wild and solitary divinity, it will immolate itself on a pyre in the middle of the unexplored ice floes of the Pole.

Literature is able to extract good from evil, and transform destruction into an exalting picture. In the domestic row, vengeful destruction would also like to touch the sublime, but instead of this it falls into abjection, confusion and spite. This degradation can make the row infernal by inciting the protagonists to sink even deeper into malignity: since I have lost my dignity, I might as well surrender all appearances of acting well, and instead make the most of a shameful, unrestrained line of conduct (what I mean here by dignity, is what makes us still have some value for others, what shows we have a place in the world of others).

And when, in the row, aggressive desire is turned back on oneself, it sinks into blackmail and abjection: 'I'm going to kill myself, and you'll have my death on your conscience!' There is a high price to pay for the sake of realizing the ideal of pathetic grandeur: words have to be matched by action. Maurice Leenhardt (a pastor, then an ethnographer, who spent twenty-five years among the Kanaks of New Caledonia) came across several cases of *suicide passionel*. In his book *Do Kamo*, he shows, through these examples, that the Kanaks, though they are so different from us in certain respects, are no less a prey to amorous passion. One woman who was betrayed by her lover, a slave to the grief of a dependence that tore her apart, set herself free by taking her own life.[6] By following through to the very end the rage and sense of annihilation that gripped her, she acquired the immense power to haunt the unfaithful man and occupy his heart for ever. Here, in reality – and not just in the fiction of horror stories – we find the inverting of impotence into the omnipotence of the spectre.

I have emphasized the analogies between the infernal couple in Mary Shelley's novel and the bad side of a couple relationship. But in reality, not just these, but all human relations contain the seed of the crisis which *Frankenstein* carries through to its highest pitch of intensity. The fact is that our fundamental propensity to exist as a complete whole clashes with the fact that in order to exist, we must exist in the mind of at least a few other people; we need to occupy a defined place in a shared world. The sensations, the material or mental objects which we desire, cannot in themselves fulfil us; if they sustain us, it is also invariably on condition that they allow us indirectly to occupy a certain place in the mind of others. So, doomed to incompleteness and the hazards of dependency, we strive by every possible means to escape the walls of our prison.

Love (between parents and children or between people of the same generation) is one of these means, and this is why it is fundamentally ambiguous; on the one hand it checks the desire to be everything and enables us to attain some degree of self-effacement for the sake of the beloved person; on the other it happens to be in the service of the desire for self-totalization, and the person who loves expects the beloved to actualize and complete his or her own existence.

Now, whatever bond of love or affection we have with someone else, this bond never leads us entirely to renounce this latter ambition, nor does it ever allow us quite to satisfy it: the other always remains an other. He does not share the feelings which we bring to him. Or else he responds to them, then his attitude changes. Or else, on a more banal level, he is not as we would like him to be. Moreover, by confronting us with the uncertainty and limits of our power, the search for reciprocity makes us acutely aware of our dependency. Reciprocity requires that we be pleasant, that we present an aspect of ourselves that finds favour, that we take up positions which suit the other. Even if we do this, we are still exposed to failure! Finally, even if we acknowledge that the other responds to our desires and is good for us, in the end it is he or she, not ourselves, to whom we are indebted for this good.

We must acknowledge that, in these conditions, hatred presents advantages that love does not offer. Hatred serves the undertaking of occupying the mind of the other, and it can get there by itself, without having to depend upon his or her consent. By hating, I can enjoy the power of affirming myself absolutely and unconditionally. I can haunt the other with my hatred and impose myself upon him as the image of the beloved possesses the lover; in this case it is the other who depends on me, not me on him. So, only hatred can provide the dream of love with its complete fulfilment.

In his *Memoirs from the House of the Dead*, Dostoevsky relates the episode which had brought one of his fellow prisoners to the penal colony.[7] This story gives a clear example of how a human being, in the grip of love but incapable of facing up to the incompleteness and dependence it entails, becomes driven, despite himself, to hatred and destruction.

The story takes place in a poor village. An old man, who is well respected and quite comfortably off, has a daughter of marriageable age, Akulka. A young man, Filka, has business dealings with the father. He demands what is owed to him, and taunts the old fellow with these words: 'I won't have your Akulka: I've slept with her without the need of that'. Filka, for some unknown reason, is bent on tarnishing Akulka's reputation. She is given a long, severe beating by her parents, and the trader to whom the old man had planned to marry his daughter no longer wants her. During this period, Filka, who has enough money to go on a spree, gets drunk from morning till night.

With his daughter dishonoured, the father finally gives her in marriage to a poor boy, one of Filka's drinking companions. The latter is astonished to discover on the wedding night that Akulka in fact turned out to be 'as innocent as could be'. He therefore reproves Filka for his slanders, but Filka, who is cleverer than the new bridegroom, convinces him that in reality he has been duped. The man beats his young wife and drinks.

Filka, for his part, goes on even wilder binges until the day when he is to be taken to the barracks to join the army, and is sobered up. Then, surrounded by the villagers whom he will leave behind, Filka declares to Akulka that he loves her, and asks her forgiveness for all the harm he has done her. The young woman answers Filka with unexpected kindness. The thing is that she loves him, too. This confession is the last straw in her husband's humiliation; he takes Akulka into a field and cuts her throat.

We could compare this story with Tolstoy's novel *The Kreutzer Sonata*, which depicts the torments of a jealous husband who ends up killing his wife. The social milieus to which the characters belong are as different as their passions are alike. In both stories, we see a man driven to hatred by the dependency of love. *How can we bear it that the object necessary to fulfilment of oneself can be someone other than one's self?* This question is as insoluble for Filka as it is for Tolstoy's character (and probably also for Tolstoy himself). Alcohol, by contrast, can refuse Filka nothing. He finds in it an oceanic satiety, and besides, by making his drinking bouts public, he shows everyone that his self-gratification is dependent on no one. For him (and in reality, too, for millions of men), this is the royal road to manly affirmation. With a woman, what can you do? However much you beat her, she is still *someone else*. Yes, it is impossible for a man either to renounce this woman's body (the call of the flesh, as Tolstoy well knew, is much stronger than will power) or to stop it from being that of an *other* person – an other person who has her own desires, and on whom the man's desire compels him to depend. For Filka and for Tolstoy's character, existing means existing as a unit, quite entire – so that, unable either to escape the intensity of their desire or to prevent it from binding them to someone else, their love turns to hatred. And to cross the barrier of their impotence, their affirmation of themselves finds its only way out in self-destruction, violence and cruelty.

5

Pity for the Monster

'Since I am unable to make people like me, since no one takes pity on me, I might as well make myself thoroughly hated and, in this way, take pleasure in the suffering and terror that I bring about,' the monster seems to say. The author of the novel, for her part, appears to be delivering a moral message in answer to the sorry sequence of events which condemns the monster to malignity: deeply distressed because of its physical repulsiveness and the rejections of others, the monster is a victim, and deserves from the reader the pity denied it by Victor.

Such ideas which combine in the narrative design correspond to what I shall call the 'triangle of moral relations'. This triangle is a way of inscribing interpersonal relations within a defined form, a framework which seals an alliance between *sensibility* (an expansion of the self as a resonance with an external reality) and the fundamental *moral principle* of equality and justice (treating every human being as an *alter ego*).

The 'triangle of moral relations' became constituted and diffused in the second half of the eighteenth century.[1] Now, more than ever before, it organizes our perceptions and moral reactions. The model which makes possible this alliance between the spontaneous movement of sensibility and the demands of morality has been borrowed from fictional narratives and, more particularly, from the theatre. It derives from a moralization of spectacle. On the stage there are two characters: the villain and the innocent victim; the oppressor and the oppressed. The spectator forms the triangle's third apex. It is the spectator who reacts to the behaviour of the villain with an indignation which demonizes him; and he or she responds to the victim's distress with a compassion which idealizes him. The spectator identifies with the latter, whereas he believes himself to have nothing in common with the villain. Thus, thanks to the double axis along which the deployment of his feelings is called upon, the third party is delivered from the ambivalence which is naturally attached to them. And so he is rid of his bad feelings, which are transferred in their entirety on to the character of the villain. However, he keeps their energy, and since this energy is now converted into indignation, it has become legitimate. The dualism of the picture offered to him allows him to enjoy the exalting feeling of *being simultaneously undivided and good* – a synthesis which exerts an irresistible attraction over all human beings.

The triangle of moral relations is very much our business. It leads us – this is what makes it so obliging, even dangerous – to confuse the principle of morality with our real make-up. In the principle which defined it, the distinction between good and evil is clear and evident; the concept of what is just and right can be marked off without any ambiguity. But in our real being, on the other hand, it is not possible entirely to separate black and white, the wheat from the chaff. Of course, it is good to wish to be good; but it is not good to believe that, in order to be good, one should and can liberate oneself from that ambivalence of which I spoke in relation to the 'price of monotheism'. This ambivalence, as I stressed, is a *constitutive* part of our being. To believe that one should and can liberate oneself from it is, therefore, to idealize oneself and to believe that one is what in reality one is not. It is, moreover, to project on to the reality of others the effects of our own confusion, which prevents us from thinking about this reality as it requires to be thought about (and how can we improve things if we do not see them as they are?).

A young man I know told me about seeing the film *The Elephant Man* for the first time as a child. The deformed individual who gives the film its title, a being who has appeared from nowhere and who emits inarticulate sounds, had at first had a nightmare effect on

him. But when he saw the film again a few years later, nothing like
that occurred; he felt touched by the bottomless grief of this
appallingly afflicted creature, and his heart went out to him. In a
comparable manner, Frankenstein's creature can arouse pity after
it has provoked terror. The pity is a sensitivity to injustice and the
desire to make it good. But the pity inspired by the distress and
grief of a fictional character goes beyond a reaction to injustice.
From terror to pity involves a reversal. But there is also (albeit in a
less obvious way) something that remains: the ascendancy of the
bad infinite. *The bad infinite manifests itself at first as a force of
destruction, then, when the character is seen from within, as an abyss of
distress.* The object of terror and the object of pity are then
symmetrical, like two mirror-images – like Yahweh and Job. And
they send out the same appeal to identification.

Children learn first to *prompt* pity, and only later to *have* pity. The
child spontaneously plays with the power to prompt pity, a power
which is liable to act strongly upon the adult, and to overturn the
relation of weak to strong in his favour. He or she is in the role of
Job, but a Job to whom God, struck with compassion, would bring
comfort. Making a show of his pain allows the child to attract the
benefits of the protective omnipotence with which he endows his
parents; and at the same time to take some discreet revenge on
them by making them feel the weight of what they owe him. Thus,
when the child reaches the point of *having* pity, this feeling is
backed up by the earlier experience of *prompting* pity. Of course, it
is not reducible to this initial experience; but access to the moral
dimension of pity does not thereby eliminate the underlying source.
Having pity on the Elephant Man or on Frankenstein's creature is
a matter of moral feeling, but it is also, in a more confused way, a
sense of resonance within oneself of powerful waves emanating
from some unfathomable pain.

The benevolence of parents in relation to their children is
manifest in all kinds of everyday circumstances which do not involve
either distress, immense distance or pity. Pity is, one could say, a
form of benevolence, but a very particular one. Benevolence circulates through ordinary relations and relative issues (it can be
exercised between persons of equal status, who are secure and have

nothing to worry about). Pity, on the other hand – like cruelty – requires some deep suffering, something absolute at stake and a vertical distance between the two protagonists (the call to pity resonates between animal and human, victim and tormentor, slave and master, child and parent, man and God). It is therefore not surprising that stories (be they religious, heroic or merely meant to entertain) more readily stage scenes of pity or cruelty than of blander forms of benevolence or malevolence; why would stories confine themselves to the comparative when they are quite at liberty to use the superlative?

It is the fount of limitlessness evoked by objects of terror or pity which explains why representations of wretchedness can be a source of pleasure. In the eighteenth century, there was a great deal of puzzling over the paradox of a certain pleasure procured by the representation of what, in reality, was in fact very painful. We are going to pause for a moment over an author of this period, Edmund Burke, whose observations might well form an altogether appropriate preface for *Frankenstein*. Later on we shall come back to what is pleasurable about the pity inspired by the monster.

Burke is best known, at least in France, for his *Reflections on the Revolution in France*, a work in which he professes opinions which are very far removed from the enthusiasm evidenced by another witness to the period, Mary Wollstonecraft, Mary Shelley's mother. A good thirty years earlier, in 1757, Burke had published his *The Sublime and Beautiful* – a work in which he writes notably that ugliness is quite compatible with the sublime, especially when it is of a kind to arouse terror. Burke counterposes the straightforward pleasure which excludes terror against what he designates 'delight', a kind of pleasure which is exhibited in relation to pain. Concerning the representation of wretchedness in tragedy, Burke points out that the 'delight' which it brings about has usually been attributed 'first, to the comfort we receive in considering that so melancholy a story is no more than a fiction; and next, to the contemplation of our own freedom from the evils which we see represented'.[2] Had Burke written his book a few years later, he would have been able to add another explanation to the ones he lists: by arousing pity, the representation of unjust wretchedness swells the hearts of spectators and makes them feel better. But Burke would probably have rejected this explanation, like others before it, since for him the representation of violence constitutes *in itself* a source of 'delight'. Suffering and destruction, he argues, are the consequence of forces of incomparable violence: 'the idea of pain, in its highest degree, is much stronger than the highest degree of pleasure'. Indeed, mere pleasure is, by definition, in accordance with our nature; the forces at play in what is pleasant are not disproportionate in relation to our own. By comparison: 'pain is always inflicted by a power in some way superior, because we never submit to pain willingly, so that strength, violence, pain and terror, are ideas that rush in upon the mind together'. This recalls Balzac's remark in *The Lily of the Valley*: 'Pain is infinite, joy has its limits.' For Burke, therefore, the sublime, with the delight it brings about, is not what it will be for Kant: the sense of our destiny within a divine order. According to Burke, the sublime has terror as its essential principle. It is a delight in an unleashing of forces. It requires darkness, infinity and destruction. The sublime 'comes upon us in the gloomy forest, and in the howling wilderness, in the form of the lion, the tiger, the panther, or rhinoceros'. We find it in the Book of Job, with its 'magnificent description' of the Leviathan. The sublime erupts in *Paradise Lost*, particularly when Milton depicts Death:

> . . . The other shape –
> If shape it might be called that shape had none
> Distinguishable in member, joint, or limb;
> Or substance might be called that shadows seemed,
> For each seemed either – black it stood as night,
> Fierce as ten Furies, terrible as hell,
> And shook a dreadful dart: what seemed his head
> The likeness of a kingly crown had on.[3]

In view of Burke's quotations from the Book of Job (man annihilated in the face of the Almighty) and from *Paradise Lost* (the evocation of Chaos, of infinite space, of Death, of Satan's revolt), I would be prepared to believe that he sees the sublime as a kind of delight in the self linked to the desire for identification with limitlessness – particularly since he writes about the ambition which drives us to prevail over our own kind in these terms: 'and this swelling is never more perceived, nor operates with more force, than when without danger we are conversant with terrible objects, the mind always claiming to itself some part of the dignity and importance of the things which it contemplates'.[4] This is Burke extending an observation which he has read in the treatise *On the Sublime* attributed to Longinus (probably written in the first century AD): 'For the true sublime, by some virtue of its nature, elevates us: uplifted with a sense of proud possession, we are filled with joyful pride, as if we had ourselves produced the very thing we heard.'[5]

I must beware, however, of attributing my own ideas to Burke. For it is I who regard what has been called the sublime as a form of narcissistic fulfilment: a spectacle or a text deploys a figure of completion, of omnipotence, of infinitude, and we are carried away by it (that is to say, compelled to identify with that figure); it evokes an origin or a destination which magnetizes us, prompting our sense of existing to be affirmed beyond the bounds which, in everyday life, keep us within the relative and bind us to others.

This kind of excitement is not confined to Westerners; human beings, as a general rule, are open to forms of seduction which are to varying extents pernicious, and to the appeal to identification sent out by figures of limitlessness (contemporary Chinese cinema, for example, has in no time at all assimilated a certain type of tragic sublimity which was nonetheless alien to Chinese tradition: the hero's existential desolation, a solitude which is in some respects neurotic but which the director presents as something interesting, cruel and enriched by intensity). However, what Western tradition designates as the *sublime* constitutes a specific elaboration of human infinitude and the strange self-fulfilment it brings. What the sublime does is allow this fulfilment to become legitimized by connecting it to aesthetic and moral values. In Antiquity, the art of discourse was the essential vector of the sublime (the sublime of Antiquity was experienced not in solitude, but in the relation between audience and orator); in Longinus' view, a formulation whose flash of illumination makes present the warrior virtue which it evokes provides the best example of the sublime (this is why he places *The*

Iliad above *The Odyssey*). The French conception of the sublime was
to remain marked by a rhetoric of grandeur and an illustration of
virtue which bear certain imprints of virilism (obviously in Boileau,
but also in Diderot[6]). The Kantian sublime is also fairly virile, but,
first and foremost, it sees itself as the solitary affirmation of the
moral force of the individual.[7] The English sublime, in part thanks
to Milton, does not aim to be edifying. It is gloomy, violent and
wild, and its appeal is as much to women as to men. Liberated from
the veil which elsewhere tames, moralizes or ennobles it, all in all it
is more interesting, and seems to come much closer to some truth
of the soul.

Nevertheless, we shall see that with Burke there comes about a
division which allows us to avoid the impact of this truth – a division
which we must consider, for from that time on it has played a
fundamental part in the way in which Westerners represent themselves. For if Burke does not sweeten the sublime, if he does not
hide its connection with destruction, he still locates himself far
short of Milton: it is only in the *aesthetic* emotions of the soul that
he recognizes this fondness for destruction. With Burke, the
domain of aesthetics and literature becomes what it has always been
ever since: a realm in which the bad infinite can express itself quite
freely *without its evidence thereby entailing the slightest consequence at the
philosophical level* (if the bad infinite has re-entered the realm of the
conceivable in our own day, this is due to psychoanalysis, not to
philosophy). Burke sees clearly that human beings are no angels,
since they are likely to enjoy the most distressing spectacles (their
fellows in the throes of suffering, a city engulfed by flames).[8]
Reading Burke brings to mind Pierre Loti's report on the taking of
Hué (which gave him a few problems with the Navy Ministry): 'The
villages of the hinterland were a blaze of red flames and black
smoke. . . . And everyone rejoiced to see all these fires, to see how
well things were turning out, how quickly this country was being set
alight. We were aware of nothing else, and every feeling was
absorbed into this amazing joy in destruction.' Fleeing from the
fire, the Vietnamese ran into the open, only to be sprayed with
bullets; then, after the shooting, amid the general excitement, the
wounded were finished off by being bayonetted or bludgeoned.[9]

Burke, however, makes no connection between flames and war. He draws no anthropological consequence from the pleasures of destruction. This is because Burke is an Enlightenment mind: his conception of the human being has its place under the dual patronage of theism and scientific explanation. Theism implies an infinite, but a positive – even providential – infinite. As for his interest in empirical research, this leads to a conception of human passions in which the infinite plays no part. Here we are a long way from those seventeenth-century Augustinian moralists for whom self-regard, left to its own devices, is boundless. Even if for Burke the idea of pride as it was conceived some decades earlier has not disappeared, for him, as for the majority of eighteenth-century philosophers, self-love tends to come down to *self-preservation*. A 'passion' which is, in the end, more utilitarian than passionate, since the self involved here refers not to the soul but to the body.

The attraction to the beautiful is linked to social passions, Burke tells us, and an interest in the sublime is linked to self-preservation. This symmetry is more apparent than real. For once it is acknowledged that a sense of the beautiful contributes to social relations (and primarily relations between the sexes), we expect Burke to demonstrate how an interest in the sublime contributes to self-preservation. But Burke tells us instead that if the sublime always arouses a feeling of terror, this is because it presents us with a picture of what endangers *physical* self-preservation. Burke's anthropology, as we can see, does not allow him to imagine that representations of destruction exalt the *soul* through illustrations of its own boundlessness. Burke is neither Milton (who imagined the bad infinite) nor Sade.

To conclude our discussion of Burke and get back to *Frankenstein*, let us say that the author of *A Philosophical Inquiry into the Origin of Our Ideas of the Sublime and Beautiful* helps us to recognize that the terror or pity experienced before the monster is mingled with the enjoyment of the limitlessness and the omnipotence to which it gives form; but that, as if it were necessary to limit the scope of potentially unpleasant and worrying observations, Burke introduces a hiatus between aesthetic activities (where the bad infinite is expressed without any restriction) and human nature (which is supposed to be fundamentally positive). This division, which persists today, is one which I challenge; and I maintain, rather, that fictional narratives speak to us of what we are.

It remains to show how the monster, under cover of the *moral* pity it prompts in the reader, also offers him or her something that responds to a *fulfilling* pity, a pity of identification.

First, the story of its life which Frankenstein's creature narrates shows us that in its own way, it is no less Promethean than Victor. Victor created its body, but the monster shaped its own mind.

There are several ways of being one's own origin. By making his creature, Victor wishes to realize or make himself – rather as Rousseau, imagining himself as Émile's private tutor, makes or remakes himself. *Robinson Crusoe*, the only Bible Rousseau imposes on Émile, gives him the model of an entrepreneurial man who does without trade. As for the monster, it does without both trade and tutor. We shall see how, while remaining anchored in the no-man's-land of the savage state, it attains to a social state which owes nothing to society, and acquires all on its own an awareness of self, of language, reading, knowledge and refined feeling. It will thus become a reflection of Victor, one which is simultaneously a resemblance and an inversion.

An inverted reflection: its external aspect presents the all-too-visible image of the invisible guilt which, unknown to those close to him, gnaws at Victor's soul. Conversely, the fine and noble qualities known to them are there, in the heart of his creature, but remain hidden.

A reflected resemblance: the two characters offer the same violent contrast between interior and exterior, a discontinuity, a rift which breaks all social bonds for them and, at the same time, gives them up to the higher passion of being at one's own origin.

The monster is at its own origin first because – unlike the rest of us who began by being babies – it is present at the awakening of itself, of its sensations, of its awareness of the world around it. It embodies the fantasy of being born an adult. This is certainly a pleasant and infantile daydream, but one which, in the eighteenth century, becomes combined with more serious preoccupations.

These are stories of children quite isolated from any society, in whom human nature would be revealed in its inborn integrity (for example, Ducray-Duminil's novel, *Victor ou l'enfant de la forêt* (1797), which was extremely successful[10]). These are the scholarly pictures of the earliest development of the human mind as painted by Locke, Condillac or Buffon. Buffon has the first man utter these words: 'I did not know what I was, where I was, or whence I came. I opened my eyes. What an abundance of sensation!'[11] This is the same style of speech which the monster adopts at the beginning of its autobiography: 'A strange multiplicity of sensations seized me, and I saw, felt, heard, and smelt at the same time.' Although these sensations are muddled at first, they are nonetheless immediately – and as if miraculously – accompanied by self-awareness. It is quite probable that Mary Shelley turned to Locke in order to outline this picture of the monster as a new Adam discovering nature and its beauties.[12] However, she might also have been inspired by reading *Paradise Lost.* Indeed, Milton had already (in 1667 – that is, more than twenty years before Locke) placed the same wondering testimony in the mouths of Adam and Eve. He has Eve say:

> That day I oft remember, when from sleep
> I first awaked, and found myself reposed,
> Under a shade on flowers, much wondering where
> And what I was, whence thither brought, and how.

Recalling the same moment of self-being, Adam says:

> . . . about me round I saw
> Hill, dale, and shady woods, and sunny plains.
> And liquid lapse of murmuring streams; . . .[13]

Adam is, however, aware of the difficulty of bearing witness to his own origin:

> For man to tell how human life began
> Is hard; for who himself beginning knew?[14]

The monster is likewise at the origin of itself in the sense that it is its own tutor. Having experienced the horror it inspires in human beings, it finds refuge in 'a low hovel' joined to 'a cottage of a neat and pleasant appearance'. It finds a chink in the wall 'through which the eye could just penetrate'. It sees the inhabitants of the house, a blind old man and a pair of young people. These three characters, endowed with every quality, form a small idyllic society. Filled with feelings of admiration and envy, the monster spends months observing this ideal epitome of humanity. Thus it fuels its intellectual development, its moral sense and its culture. By good fortune, several works fall into its hands: *Paradise Lost* (not unreasonably, the monster feels close to Milton's Satan); Plutarch's *Lives* (a standard classic of the day, but also favourite reading for two great reprobates: the ageing Rousseau, solitary and persecuted, and Karl Moor, the hero of Schiller's *The Robbers*); the *Sorrows of Werther* (the monster is obviously a kind of Werther, rejected, not by Charlotte, but by its creator and by society). Add to these emblematic works the young cottager's reading aloud of Volney's *Ruins of Empires* (the author was a friend of Condorcet, and a disciple of Holbach and Helvetius).

It is easy to understand that the monster gives pleasure to the reader when it presents itself as a new Adam and an autodidact. But what about when it appears as an outcast, as the rejected and shunned voyeur of a couple whom it envies (the young cottagers, Victor and his fiancée Elisabeth)? Nevertheless, we shall see that in this wretched position the monster illustrates a desire which is very close to the one of being (or being present at) one's own origin: the desire to be *undivided* (in the literal sense of the word: not split). To make this clearer, the simplest thing is to take a quick detour around two works later than that of Mary Shelley, in which the same fantasy unfolds and likewise prompts pity, not to say tears: *The Little Mermaid* and *Toilers of the Sea*.

In Hans Christian Andersen's tale, the heroine is a sea-sprite who longs to become a human being. She could achieve this were she to win the love of a man. She loves a young prince, whom she has saved from a shipwreck (but the prince is unaware that she was the one who saved him). What prevents the little mermaid from being recognized by him is not, as in the monster's case, her physical appearance; she is pretty, and she has swapped her fish's tail for a pair of legs. But she has paid for these legs with her voice. She will never be able to tell the prince who she is and what she has done for him, or speak of her love for him. The young man will marry someone else. The sea-sprite knows that her failure means her death. For one last time, before she dissolves into the foam, she contemplates the couple who embody her ideal, and who do not see her.

The little mermaid has not been recognized, she remains cut off from the human race. For her the pain of this is agonizing. But for the reader, this rejection and death open the door to the dream of an existence experienced in the infinite. Mingled with the compassion which he or she feels for this unhappy fate, there is a delicious sense of an *I* which, unrecognized and unidentified, *escapes the limitations imposed by the bonds between individuals*, and enjoys its own infinity. This feature – a character's inability to be recognized, transmuted into delight – had already appeared in its most literal form in Schiller's play *The Robbers* (1781).[15] Karl Moor, a hero who is at once virtuous and outlawed, finds himself repeatedly in the presence of his father or of Amalia, the young woman he loves, but neither of them recognizes him (in the strict sense of the word). Nowadays, this lack of verisimilitude would strike us as ridiculous. But for Schiller's contemporaries, it added to the painful grandeur of the character, and to his absolute character, in the etymological meaning of the term, which is to say: freed from all bonds. The compassion which he thereby inspired in the play's audience contributed to their delight.

Gilliatt, the hero of Victor Hugo's novel *Toilers of the Sea*, the Gilliatt in whom Victor Hugo saw a Job–Prometheus, is a bit like the little mermaid, a character bound to the depths of the sea. But the gulf which separates him from the young woman he loves is above all a social gulf – a distance which will prove as unbridgeable as the one that separates the little mermaid or Frankenstein's creature from humanity. At the end of the novel, we see Gilliatt sitting on a rock as the tide comes in. He is waiting for it to submerge and drown him. At the point when only his face remains above the water, he sees a ship sail away into the distance, and on it, he surmises, is the young woman for whose sake he is sacrificing himself – the young woman and her fiancé going off to start a new life.

How many adolescents have shed tears as they read the final pages of *Toilers of the Sea* or *The Little Mermaid*! How many saw themselves in the place of the rejected character, similarly overwhelmed by his or her grief – but, unlike the experience of Gilliatt or the little mermaid, giving way to this oceanic dissolution in a delightful and limitless expansion of themselves!

Moving from the dream to its realization involves renouncing the infinitude which haloes it. Had she been loved, the little mermaid would have had to renounce her *undivided* being in order to become a woman, to become her companion's other *half*. And Gilliatt likewise would have had to give up his titanic stature and be reduced to a good bourgeois husband. By failing to realize the dream of love (which they nonetheless see through to its very end), these two characters give the reader an exalting sense of a twofold integrity: reparation for the other and reparation for oneself. The reader would like to put right the unhappy outcome of the story by making good the harm suffered by the character who prompts his or her compassion (this is the moral side of the pity). Nevertheless, in a confused way, the reader is gratified by this very outcome which is deplored, for it offers an invaluable compensation for the non-fulfilment of his or her own wishes: like the mermaid and like Gilliatt, the young reader thereby escapes the alternative, the splitting involved in the difference between the sexes, and he or she can enjoy the satisfaction of being able to dream of love without this entailing any abandonment of infantile completeness.

Like Gilliatt and the little mermaid, Frankenstein's creature offers the reader the satisfaction of a figure of completeness – with the difference that it pushes it even further than do the two characters imagined by Andersen and Victor Hugo. It does not merely embody, as they do, the refusal of sexual difference (it has been created, not procreated); but also the refusal of the even more fundamental split between the living and the dead (in this it is comparable to its creator searching for the secret of life in vaults and charnel-houses). The monster, as we have seen, is a species of revenant or living dead; its very appearance bears this out. What it presents to others is not a face but a blazon of destruction. This excludes it for ever from the society of men; but also allows it to preserve the infinitude of the spectre.

Thus rejected, the monster is excused from having to be nice to others. Now – as we saw when we compared the respective advantages of love and hate – being nice means internalizing the split between oneself and the other; it means limiting oneself in order to make room for the other, and is therefore a kind of renunciation of being whole. The monster's malignity is a kind of affirmation of its wholeness.

Rejected, the monster remains unnameable: all naming sets limits. In one of the key scenes in the novel the monster emerges, not from its tomb, but from its hovel, in an attempt to be recognized as a human being by the old man who lives in the cottage. The encounter begins well: since he is blind, the person whom the monster has chosen in this desperate bid is not at all frightened by his visitor, and shows it the greatest kindness. Unfortunately, the young people, who had gone out, return earlier than expected. At the very moment when the old man asks the monster the question: 'Who are you?', the door opens, the young people are terror-stricken, and the monster, once more reduced to fury and despair, can only flee. Who are you? – a question which, for it, has no answer.

H. P. Lovecraft employed a variant of this scene for one of his horror stories, *The Outsider*.[16] The narrator is a being who lives alone in the cavernous darkness of a tomblike castle. In order to emerge from this hole, this non-place, he undertakes a difficult ascent, at the end of which he reaches not, as he had supposed, the top of a tower, but merely ground level. Then, walking, he reaches a dwelling where there are lights and a festive gathering is under way. Through the French windows he sees a happy group of people, which he perhaps thinks of joining. But hardly has he stepped inside when they all run away, terrified. Then the narrator comes face to face with a formless and repulsive monster, a mass of putrid flesh. He reaches out to push this ghastly vision aside, and his hand encounters the cold surface of a mirror!

The reader of the story participates in the narrator's undertaking, discovering with his or her own vision the staging of the tale. At the end, the mirror discloses a kind of Hallowe'en character, and it is as if, with the narrator as intermediary, the reader himself were clad in a particularly convincing fancy dress. Reduced to nothing, the story's narrator can only go back to his catacombs. No doubt the reader feels pity for him; however, he or she is spared the pain which the character is imagined to feel. What is more, when the reader sees the reflected image of this solitary being unconfined by any bounds, what he or she feels – to return to Burke's chosen term – is delight. The pitiable monsters of Lovecraft and Mary Shelley are pernicious, morbid and depressing; yet, to the extent that the reader takes them in as fiction and locates them in the space of play, the figures of the absolute which these characters deploy brings this reader closer to the sources of his or her own physical vitality.

The monster imagined by Lovecraft, the victim of a brutally unjust fate, is, like Frankenstein's creature, a new Job. At the end of his quest, there is a revealing confrontation – not with the Leviathan or with Yahweh, but with his own boundlessness. This confrontation offers no answer to the problem of evil, any more than does the one between Job and God. But it shows that pain brings us much closer to infinitude than happiness does. As Burke wrote – and precisely before taking the Book of Job as his example: 'the idea of pain, in its highest degree, is much stronger than the highest degree of pleasure'. It has to be acknowledged that dark, 'negative', depressing ideas can exert an irresistible seductive power over us – an attraction with which 'positive', pleasant and constructive (therefore relative and limited) ideas cannot compete. Malice, dissatisfaction, and a liking for depressing ideas derive from the same source.

6

Thought and Reason
versus Literature and Passion

Mary Shelley feels compassion for her monster. When it pleads its cause before its creator, she places in its mouth arguments to which she herself adheres. 'I was benevolent and good; misery made me a fiend. Make me happy, and I shall again be virtuous.' And further on: 'Believe me, Frankenstein: I was benevolent; my soul glowed with love and humanity; but am I not alone, miserably alone? . . . If the multitude of mankind knew of my existence, they would do as you do, and arm themselves for my destruction. Shall I not then hate them who abhor me?'

These arguments became widespread in the second half of the eighteenth century as a means of reconciling the thesis of the natural goodness of man with what began to be known about the 'noble savage' in terms that did not fit with such idealization: 'All the painters of savage customs place no benevolence in their pictures,' wrote the Abbé Raynal. 'But has not prejudice made them confuse natural character with a *resentful antipathy*? . . . In retaliation, they have become harsh and cruel towards us.' The cruelties of which the Europeans complain are in fact only a reaction to their odious conduct.[1] This argument ensured that the picture of human misdeeds, however overwhelming, did not contradict the thesis of natural goodness; the malignity of the Europeans is not taken into account, since they are denatured; nor is that of the savages, since it is only a reaction to the behaviour of the colonizers. And even by acknowledging that the savages' customs were cruel *before* the Westerners' arrival, their perfectibility assures us that a process of civilization and education will restore them to a natural goodness which has been obscured only by ignorance. After all, as Diderot wrote to Sophie Volland: 'Nature has not made us wicked; it is by bad education, bad example and bad legislation that we are corrupted.'[2] 'Men of the same society are naturally at peace,' Saint-Just was to say in 1793, arguing that man is only 'made wretched and corrupted by the insidious laws of domination'.[3] But as a consequence, in this world where everyone is fundamentally good, evil can be introduced – as in an earthly paradise – only by beings who, beneath their human appearance, are in reality diabolical. 'I am sorry there is no hell for the abominable corrupters of those children,'[4] wrote Diderot. Contrary to the way humanist optimism sees itself, it does not avoid dualism.

In the view of the poet Shelley, of Mary and her father William Godwin, and many other progressives of the time, the thesis of natural goodness carries all the more force for being a necessary condition for the belief that a better society will bring about human happiness. Indeed, Enlightenment philosophy had to uphold this thesis in order to transfer the idea of Salvation from the religious to the political sphere. If original sin is necessary to the Christian doctrine of Salvation, political redemption requires instead that evil have its source within existing society (and in certain diabolical individuals), but not within the human soul in general. Social injustice and obscurantism are all of a piece; so Volney was to write in his *Catéchisme du citoyen* – a kind of secular Ten Commandments based on natural law – that 'the true original sin' was ignorance[5] (while for the Church, the sin had, rather, been that of eating from 'the tree of knowledge'). There could be no clearer affirmation of the promotion of the *subject of knowledge* to the rank of model human being. Progress is therefore the way to the new Salvation, happiness in this world.

Being exempted from original sin means being rid of the bad infinite. It means being endowed by nature with the sense of one's own existence, and being sufficiently endowed with it to enjoy an untroubled sense of oneself. It means satisfying the desire for self-preservation thanks to a clear grasp of what is in one's interest.[6] It means not depending on someone else in order to be oneself (such a dependence could only be the effect of artificial passions produced by a denatured society).

The political progressivism of the Enlightenment is professed in an exemplary manner by William Godwin in the work that made him famous: *Enquiry Concerning Political Justice and Its Influence on General Virtue and Happiness* (1793). Godwin set out his aims in this work: 'The method to be pursued ... shall be, first, to take a concise survey of the evils existing in political society; secondly, to show that these evils are to be ascribed to public institutions; and thirdly, that they are not the inseparable condition of our existence, but admit of removal and remedy.'[7] Further on, he points out that in a just society, jealousy and hatred would cease to prevail, since they are only the results of injustice. Despite his reservations over certain aspects of Godwin's thought which struck him as utopian, Benjamin Constant admired the English author. And in the appendix which he added to his translation of *Political Justice*, Constant himself wrote: 'day by day passion loses its dominion, and what it loses, reason gains'.[8] The Godwinian School – as it was then called in England – militated for a social politics of the left; while in the view of its adversaries, the Godwinians' progressivism came down to a recognition that anyone is deserving so long as he is poor, and their politics, if put into practice, would lead only to an increase in crime.[9]

This chapter is concerned to show, on the basis of a *roman à thèse* by William Godwin, how the inner spring of malice, which has no place in the militant *thought* of Mary Shelley's father, surfaces in the unthought *narration* – how, in other words, what the *subject of knowledge* has chased out of the door is smuggled back in by the *subject of existence* to whom the narrative thread addresses itself.

The French are not familiar with Godwin, yet, in late-eighteenth- and early-nineteenth-century England, he enjoyed a prestige comparable to that of Sartre in twentieth-century France. Godwin, too, was a philosopher and novelist, and was similarly preoccupied with social injustice and the sufferings of his fellow men. In 1794, a year after *Political Justice*, Godwin published a novel, *Things as they are: or The Adventures of Caleb Williams*. This novel was an enormous success in England, but also in France, through both its translation in 1796 and its stage adaptation in 1798 (later, Balzac was to express his admiration for 'the celebrated Godwin's masterpiece'). As we shall see as we get to know *Caleb Williams, Frankenstein* owes a great deal to Godwin's novel.

In writing *Caleb Williams,* it was Godwin's intention to illustrate the ideas which he had developed in *Political Justice* as a good disciple of Holbach, Helvetius and Rousseau, and as an enthusiastic witness to the French Revolution. But what is disturbing for a reader today is that *Caleb Williams* seems much rather to contradict these optimistic ideas. Whereas *Political Justice* constantly presupposes the natural goodness of man, the novel shows us characters fettered by bonds which are both destructive and impossible to break – a hell which *Frankenstein* will remake in all its darkness, but transposing it to the register of the horror story. Thus, for William Godwin and his daughter alike, the thesis of natural goodness becomes associated with the depiction of characters moved by frenzied, hate-filled and criminal passions.

How can it be that neither Godwin nor Mary Shelley sees a contradiction in this? In Mary Shelley's case, the answer is simple: she was not setting out to illustrate ideas, but first and foremost to transmit the pleasure of fear to the reader. Protected, in a sense, by the conventions of a prevailing literary genre, she could therefore open the floodgates of violence without thereby provoking the criticism that she was presenting a pessimistic vision of human beings. She was even able to touch upon the Godwinian theme of natural goodness; as we have seen, it was not difficult to combine this theme with the malignity of the monster, once she had turned it into a victim.

Godwin, too, had made his principal character a victim; this would allow him, as it did his daughter, to give the reader the pleasure of experiencing reverberations of moral fibre while guaranteeing the pleasures of violence and destruction. All the same, unlike Mary Shelley, Godwin had no intention of offering the reader a fantastic story but, rather, a depiction of human relationships as they really are: *Things as they are,* his novel's title proclaims. Godwin sets himself apart from the Gothic novel that was then in vogue. And if he ever does aim to make the reader shiver with horror, he does not resort to medieval ruins on a stormy night to do so, but is more likely to show the terrible consequences of social injustice and prejudice. 'While one party pleads for reformation and change, the other extols in the warmest terms the existing constitution of society. It seemed as if something would be gained for the decision of this question, if that constitution were faithfully developed in its practical effects.' It is therefore a matter of showing all those who have not been able to read *Political Justice* how 'the spirit and character of the government intrudes itself into every rank of society . . . accordingly, it was proposed, in the invention of the following work, to comprehend . . . a general review of the modes of domestic and unrecorded despotism by which man becomes the destroyer of man'.[10] (Of course, one thinks of the formulation which was to become so familiar: 'man's exploitation by his fellow men').

Godwin, as he himself recounted, wrote his novel in a great feverish rush, carried away by the intensity and passion of the destructive duel enacted in it. We shall see how, even if the author believes that it merely illustrates his ideas, the narration frees itself from this guidance and fashions its own truth. Here, briefly summarized, is the plot of *Caleb Williams*.

The entire first part of the novel is taken up with a struggle to the death between two characters. One is the violent and arrogant country squire, Tyrrell, who soon becomes obsessed with an envious hatred for Falkland, another landowner who has recently settled in the area. Falkland himself possesses the finest qualities – 'a serious and sublime visionary'. After a variety of abuses which Falkland tries to ignore, the brutish Tyrrell publicly assaults him. But for Falkland – this is his only weak point – honour is everything. So now we see him racked by humiliation, loathing and a violent desire for vengeance.

Shortly afterwards, the aggressor is found dead. A man is sentenced for the crime.

Caleb Williams, a young man of humble origins, is in Falkland's service. Caleb comes round to thinking that Falkland is the real perpetrator of the crime. Caleb is intelligent and curious-minded, and he becomes increasingly consumed by his wish to uncover his master's secret. This desire is heightened when one day, having entered a small room adjoining the library, and finding in it a locked casket, Caleb is disturbed by the unexpected arrival of Falkland, who severely forbids him to enter this room.

Caleb continues to spy on his master. He sees Falkland on a stormy night wandering about like King Lear. He sees Falkland called upon to give judgement on a criminal matter resembling the murder, and unwittingly giving himself away (Caleb watches for his reactions like Hamlet watching his stepfather).

Now a fire breaks out in Falkland's house! Caleb takes advantage of it to go into the forbidden room and to force open the casket. Once again his master surprises him and, this time, can barely stop himself from shooting Caleb dead. Nevertheless, in the end Falkland is overwhelmed by his guilt and confesses to Caleb, who must, however, swear never to disclose his master's secret. The satisfaction of the young man's consuming curiosity is thus transformed into a burden as heavy as the one crushing Falkland. He tries to be free of it by escaping from his master, while the latter attempts to keep him under his control, slandering and persecuting Caleb so as to ruin his credibility before any third party. From then on, the young man's life is nothing but a succession of tribulations: imprisonment, chains, ill-treatment, escape, vagabondage, a spell with a gang of thieves, living in hiding, hopes and disillusionment, despondency, rejection and solitude.

In the end, a final tragic confrontation takes place between Caleb and a Falkland tormented by his crimes. Finally, Falkland repents for the irreparable wrongs he has done Caleb, and dies.

At the conclusion of his adventures, cast into the solitude of the reprobate, Caleb has no recourse but to write the story of his life (he is therefore the novel's narrator):

> I conceived that my story . . . would carry in it an impression of truth that few men would be able to resist . . . and, seeing in my example what sort of evils are entailed upon mankind by society as it is at

present constituted, might be inclined to turn their attention upon the fountain from which such bitter waters have been accustomed to flow.

Thus, the narrator backs up Godwin's militant intentions. From time to time, he draws lessons from events. Falkland, for example, has a sublime intellect: 'But of what use are talents and sentiments in the corrupt wilderness of human society? It is a rank and rotten soil, from which every finer shrub draws poison as it grows.' 'In some future period of human improvement, it is probable that that calamity will be in a manner unintelligible' (this being a reference to the meaning of honour and humiliation). 'How few persons would he encounter so unjust and injurious as you, if his own conduct were directed by principles of reason and benevolence?' (this with reference to the public assault on Falkland by the violent squire Tyrrell).

Here is another example. Imprisoned and in chains, the narrator achieves an inner freedom which contrasts with his master's subjugation (and that of the rich in general) to the false values of society. 'Such is man in himself considered; so simple his nature; so few his wants. How different from the man of artificial society!' Godwin, being a disciple of Rousseau, probably had in mind the author of *Reveries of a Solitary Walker*, who pronounced himself free upon his island 'cut off from the rest of the world', and convinced that he could still be so 'in the Bastille, and even in a dungeon'.[11]

Caleb is a new Job whose overwhelming fate offers the reader a meditation on the problem of evil – with two great differences by comparison with the biblical character: in the depths of his wretchedness, it is not God's omnipotence he discovers but that of society, and this, in his view, remains altogether unjustified. This is why he is simultaneously a new Prometheus bound – a Romantic Prometheus whose revolt, unlike that of the character in Aeschylus, is wholly justified.

Caleb's master has forbidden him to enter the little room with the secret casket. This is a prohibition which the story's plot legitimizes, since Caleb is in Falkland's service. But this does not prevent the young man from justifying his desire to transgress against the prohibition in these terms: 'To do what is forbidden always has its charms, because we have an indistinct apprehension of something arbitrary and tyrannical in the prohibition.' Godwin's *ideas* require Caleb to be innocent. But, for all that, the *narration* lays on him part of the responsibility for the destructive bond between him and his master.

This bond, in fact, is very much like the prototypical one in the well-known story of *Bluebeard*. In this story, however, all the emphasis is placed upon the irrepressible nature of the desire to transgress upon what is forbidden, so that the actions of the heroine who enters the locked chamber and penetrates Bluebeard's terrible secret are in no sense presented as legitimate. Perrault's version, which stays close to oral tradition, describes the torments of the heroine as she is gripped by violent curiosity – a curiosity which is no rational or justified desire, but pure passion. And the child to whom the story of *Bluebeard* is told, fascinated by the disturbing whiff of guilt which emanates from the tale, does not think of the heroine as being in the right; the tale carries too many echoes of the child's own desire to enter into a realm which his parents keep from him, and what the heroine discovers in the forbidden chamber illustrates all too well the excessive and frightening nature of the secret which he imagines as theirs. In fact, the forbidden room in which Falkland's guilty secret is concealed belongs, like Victor Frankenstein's laboratory, to the same family as Bluebeard's chamber.

The intensity which holds the reader spellbound in Godwin's novel therefore derives only very partially from the ideological struggle in which the author seeks to enlist that reader. It is primarily provided by the narrative kernel of the novel. This kernel is not reducible to ideas and, as we have just seen, is of the same kind as that of tales such as *Bluebeard*. It is likewise comparable to that of Mary Shelley's novel. Falkland and Caleb form an infernal couple whose mutual and unresolvable persecution certainly made an impression on Mary (Caleb Williams sums up his relationship to his master with these words: 'We were each of us a plague to the other'). Victor Frankenstein and Falkland, both of them sublime intellects, carry deep within themselves the weight of an unconfessable crime. For Victor and Falkland alike, *greater self-fulfilment involves the suppression of an other*: begetting, but without a partner; maintaining one's reputation, but by eliminating one's rival. The other, fatefully, returns: it is the monster, the incarnation of its creator's guilty secret; it is Caleb, the only one who knows about his master's crime. And again, the master and the creator, locked in the nightmare of the other, seek to be rid of him. This other is the living reproach to their failed desire for completeness – but also the only repository of that desire, the only soul with whom the master or the creator can share his own infinitude (which is, however, by its own definition, impossible to share). This other, in the end, succeeds where his persecutor fails, for it is he, the outcast, the vagabond, the reprobate, who, in the fathomless depths of his pain, presents to the reader the most accomplished figure of the omnipotence of the solitary, of the self undivided and devoid of an other. In this respect, the two novels make a singular contrast with the tale in the oral tradition: the heroine of *Bluebeard* is saved by her bonds of kinship (her sister Anne and her two brothers). The tale, in fact, comes out of a culture which is very different from the one that exalts the individual.

It was not just the pivot of the plot development which would have inspired Mary Shelley, but also scenes in which the hero appears as a total victim, which can provoke great waves of pity. I have mentioned, in relation to the monster, the crucial scene of its approach to the old man and his irremediable rejection. Caleb too, in the course of his tribulations, is pitied by a noble and kind old man. Seeing him as his last resort, Caleb confides in him. But when he says who he is, the old man (who, because of the slanders put about by Falkland, has heard Caleb's name mentioned in the most unfavourable terms) violently rejects the unfortunate young man. As far as he is concerned, Caleb is 'a monster with whom the very earth groaned'. Later on, in the course of an episode where a lady, who at first is very friendly, drives him away for the same reason, she tells him: 'Go, sir; I despise you. You are a monster and not a man.'

With these details from Godwin's novel in place, let us come to the relationship between ideas and narration in *Caleb Williams* and *Frankenstein.*

It is clear that Godwin's interpretation of his own novel is a way of *reducing the narration to reason* – a way which is not new: in the Christian pastoral, the depiction of catastrophes caused by worldly passions served to extol the necessity to follow the path of good. This only had to be attached to reason and good feeling, rather than to religion, for edification through storytelling to assume a secular currency. Modern interpretations of *Frankenstein* still draw on this mode of edification. It will be said, for example, that the monster is staking the claims of the heart, illustrating what happens when an extreme rationalism takes hold of people's minds (excessive trust in the Enlightenment, for example, leads from the Revolution to the Terror).[12] Or it will be said that Mary Shelley drew on her female sensibility to warn her husband against his own extremism, and gave advance notice of the risks humanity would run because of the sorcerer's apprentices of techno-science: 'Speaking the unsayable to Shelley and to mankind out of the deep knowledge of femininity and maternity, these were the issues in Mary's books,' concludes Monette Vacquin at the end of her study of *Frankenstein* and *in vitro* fertilization.[13]

According to another type of interpretation, likewise contemporary, the picture of unreason which the story offers us does not represent any danger to which it alerts us, but, rather, a normal – or at any rate unavoidable – component of ourselves. In such a case, the story invites us to accept this rather than repressing it. Thus Falkland and Victor Frankenstein embody the human being who refuses to recognize his or her own dark side, which is represented by the monster. The poor monster ought not to be rejected; instead, one should, as much as possible, love the unlovable.[14] This kind of interpretation, inspired (so it would appear) by psychoanalysis, therefore renounces the reduction of the narration to reason, and acknowledges its alterity in relation to it. Unfortunately, it goes no further. As a result, in the first place, since the interpretation is not elaborated with regard to the specific features of *Frankenstein*, it is equally applicable to all kinds of narratives (for example, *The Strange Case of Dr Jekyll and Mr Hyde*). In the second place, adhering to this type of interpretation entails the belief in a superior position consistent with recognizing realities which one would be inclined to avoid, when in fact one goes on quite plainly wanting to know nothing about these realities. In fact, read within this perspective, *Frankenstein* teaches us nothing new about ourselves, and does not alter our way of thinking – unless one regards as new the idea that there are two sides to every one of us, one being qualified as rational and the other as emotional or feeling!

In reality, here the tension between these two sides is merely a *trompe l'œil*, a façade. Behind it *Caleb Williams* and *Frankenstein* speak to us of another tension; a tension which Western history has elaborated in a particular way: the tension between the fact that there is no *self* without an order to give us a place among others; and the fact that ideally, being oneself means being God – it means being unique and boundless.

The route we have followed this far in the company of *Frankenstein* has helped us to take the measure of this tension, and to feel its force. As for *Caleb Williams*, let us bear in mind that the gap between Godwin's ideas and the narration which cannot help but fail to contain them is presented thus: while the author thinks that this tension is not inherent in the human condition, his narration suggests otherwise.

Let us be quite specific: the gap between Godwin's ideas and the narrative springs of his novel turns on the very ambiguity of the desire to free oneself from the subjection of others – a desire which is located partly on the side of *dike* (justice) and partly on the side of *hubris* (immoderation). At the level of ideas this desire becomes translated into an aspiration to justice, a conviction that each of us is worth as much as anyone else, and that anyone else is worth as much as oneself. But this desire does not stop there; beyond justice, it aims to find freedom from all others, it aims to be everything unto itself. This immoderation animates the narration which, without it, would lose what makes it compelling. At the same time, it is necessary for it not to show itself for what it is, otherwise it would rob the author and his readers of the serenity offered to them by the level of ideas – that is to say, the assurance that Caleb, and they themselves, desire nothing but justice.

Although Godwin adhered to Enlightenment philosophy, he initially intended to become a church minister, and religious studies made their mark on him. These two layers of his education are to be found in his novel: the more recent of them in his ideas, the earlier in the narration. His case – and this is what makes him so interesting to study – thus helps us to understand how, in a general way, the gulf between the writing of reason and the writing of the passions came about, and how, at the turning point between the Enlightenment and Romanticism, human infinitude became simultaneously unthinkable for reason and able to range freely in poetry, the novel, and later the cinema (hence, no doubt, Freud's comment that writers are our masters).

The seventeenth century witnessed Spinoza's extraordinary undertaking (in the third part of the *Ethics*) to conceive of a logic of the feelings and the passions. It also produced Christian moralists – Augustinians, to be precise – like Pascal, Arnauld, Nicole and La Rochefoucauld, who tussled with the *idea* of self-love. In fact, in their view, self-love does not just offer material for observation and description, it has its place in an overall conception of human beings, a conception which locates salvation in God (and not, of course, in the changing of institutions). The century of the Enlightenment shifted the emphasis from unreason, and brought it to bear upon existing society. Self-love was no longer at the mercy of a boundless desire: human beings sought only self-preservation, pursuing interests which, if clearly understood, were compatible with those of others. It is therefore no longer their essence, but social circumstances which bring them into conflict with their fellows.

Godwin was not unaware of the Jansenist conception of *amour-propre*, but he denies it any pertinence by also attributing it to the baleful influence of society:

> Virtue was never yet held in much honour and esteem in a Monarchical country. It is the inclination and the interest of courtiers and Kings, to bring it into disrepute;. . . . The philosophical system, which

affirms self-love to be the first mover of all our actions, and the full city of human virtues, is the growth of these countries.[15]

Godwin does not think about self-love in the same way as the seventeenth-century moralists, and, strictly speaking, he no longer thinks about it at all.

That, however, does not prevent him from depicting its force with as much vigour as they do. The fact is that although the cause Godwin defends is no longer that of Augustinian Christianity, the resources he places in the service of the new ideas are drawn from his early background. Godwin was the son of a dissident minister and he himself was a minister, becoming progressively distanced from the rigours of Calvinist doctrine. Like all preachers, Godwin knew that people are more easily impressed if they are shown the havoc of the Fall, sin and damnation rather than visions of Paradise. As one puritan preacher wrote in the early seventeenth century, sermons must cause their listeners to quake in fear and thorough terror of God's Law, before their barren hearts can be deemed ready to receive the sweet seed of the Gospel. Robert Bolton, the author of a work proposing solace and guidance, *Instructions for a Right Comforting Afflicted Consciences – with special antidotes against some grievous temptations* (1631), is also an advocate of shock treatment, and the God he invokes is threatening and wrathful: 'no more, nay infinitely less can any power of Man or Angel withstand the mighty Lord of Heaven and Earth when Hee is angry for Sinne'.[16]

Godwin, too, wants to make his readers quake beneath the weight of evil's depiction. Falkland's crimes pursue him like the invisible, avenging hand of God, and the process of destruction in which the novel's characters are caught up is of such crushing all-powerfulness that by necessity it compels recourse to the only remedy which, in Godwin's view, can counter it (rather as nowadays we see secular preachers evoke the intolerable reality of radical evil in order to direct those they address towards the good).

We may wonder just how much the strategy deployed by these 'hellfire preachers', whose rhetoric was familiar to Godwin, was a *deliberate* one. Indeed, they themselves ran a strong risk of being carried away by the evocations of omnipotence which ran through their sermons, and probably many of them derived pleasure from them, even unwittingly. This is why their words could often have an effect that was more crushing than edifying, and their faithful could be left confused. One moderate eighteenth-century minister described these preachers inducing their listeners to feel despair and a hatred of God.[17] Similarly, it happened that narratives intended for edification won over their readers like popular novels, through the passions that were given free rein in them – an evil which ultimately only grace could remedy – but it was the depiction of evil, not the demonstration of its remedy, which held the reader's interest.[18] In the work of eighteenth-century writers such as Richardson and Prévost, for example, the edifying project often strikes us as scarcely more than a pretext or an alibi.

But this is not the case with Godwin, who instead writes as a militant. This even accounts for the fact that the force of the story he tells owes something to one of the fundamental narratives of Christianity, the story of the Fall. What Godwin does in turning against his earlier convictions is to challenge this narrative and contradict it, to the point where his symmetrical opposition is so determined that he ends up imitating it.

I have said that the pivot of the plot in *Caleb Williams* has an affinity with the tale of *Bluebeard*. But further back still than the tale, what stimulated Godwin's imagination was the story of Adam and Eve burning to share in Yahweh's secret. In one of his youthful writings, Godwin pronounced that even God himself had no right to be a tyrant. Rejecting the dogma of original sin, in which he could see no more than an unacceptable explanation for human wretchedness, Godwin undoubtedly had in mind Yahweh's proscription ('of the tree of the knowledge of good and evil, thou shalt not eat of it: for in the day that though eatest thereof thou shalt surely die') when he made Caleb reflect upon his master's prohibition: 'we have an indistinct apprehension of something arbitrary and tyrannical in the prohibition'. Godwin therefore offers, in *Caleb Williams*, a version of the story of the forbidden fruit which inverts its meaning: the young man is not guilty in his curiosity; rather, it is his master who is, and what he keeps for himself is not a knowledge that belongs rightfully to him. It is (as in the case of *Bluebeard*) the relic of a criminal self-gratification. Out of this, however, Godwin does not develop any counter-theology, as Byron was later to do in his long poem *Cain*, where the God who forbids man from eating of the tree of knowledge is the one to blame, and Lucifer is rehabilitated. For him, going against theology is a matter of not inverting its content, but of moving away from it towards politics.

With the story of Genesis a connection was forged – a connection that is both indissoluble and untenable – between *relation to completeness* and *relation to the other*. (I cannot present a detailed analysis of the text here; I shall confine myself to demonstrating one of the conclusions which I draw from it.) The prohibition handed down by Yahweh to Adam and Eve wrenches them from the torpor of an Eden without alterity to make them desire the gratification which He, this Other, keeps for himself. But once they have crossed the frontier separating them from this gratification, new divisions replace the frontier. First, otherness is reconstituted in a different form: 'And the eyes of them both were opened, and they knew that they were naked' – from then on, they see themselves with the gaze of the other, and each of them has something to hide. Then, with death, the finiteness which characterizes the human condition makes its appearance. But the infinitude of the desire which was awakened by the forbidden fruit does not thereby disappear, it is maintained.

Christian doctrine offers a solution to this antinomy (even if in certain respects this 'solution' exacerbates the antinomy). Obey God and his law of justice, accept being only one among many. But also: know that you have been created in the image of this God who is a person and who is in himself the One and Only; participate in the infinite sacrifice that his Son made for you, and the gates to a boundless beatitude will be reopened to you. Submission to God is the source of all peace. But also: identification with God reactivates the dizziness of infinitude. For Christianity, it has been a matter of switching continually between these two extremes, of maintaining some kind of coexistence with, on the one hand, the moral principle of equality between all human beings and, on the other, the sublimity of the self's confrontation with the infinite. If this kind of association is to be more than a mere intellectual construct, religion must impregnate the social order. An order which, founded upon hierarchy and divine authority, allows each individual – at least in theory – to perceive himself or herself as having a defined place which connects him or her to others, while at the same time being connected to God and thereby enjoying, through the mediation of the clergy, a relation to completeness.

In this hierarchical and theocratic order, individualist and emancipatory conceptions, with their developing demands, could find neither enough justice nor enough self-affirmation. With the Reformation, then the Enlightenment and Romanticism, the old form of compromise between these two extremes comes apart, along with the social order upholding it. The demand for justice and the principle of equality become increasingly adopted by any juridical, political, economic and philosophical thinking which aims to be rational and appropriate to objective realities – while some part of the ideal that was invested in religion became recuperated within the political sphere. The surplus of infinitude which the political cannot absorb acquires fiction as its legitimate realm of expression (poetry, the novel and, later, film), wherein the echoes of Christian tragedy will continue to resonate.

In an age when Christianity still managed to maintain an association between ideas and narrative, Milton became the great harbinger of their imminent separation. In him, men of the Enlightenment would admire the revolutionary who justifies regicide, dreams of establishing a free republic, and would suffer no attempt to limit free expression. The Romantics would be fascinated by his theological poem *Paradise Lost*, and by the extraordinary figure of the rebel angel, in certain respects more deeply human than Adam and Eve. Already *Paradise Lost* was asking – and most forcefully – the question which Godwin (unwittingly) and Mary Shelley (perhaps more consciously) dramatized: *if God is the mirror in which I perceive and desire my own infinitude, then how will I endure being only one among many?* This is the question that visibly underlies these words which Adam addresses to God:

> Thou in thyself art perfect, and in thee
> Is no deficience found; not so is man,

> But in degree – the cause of his desire
> By conversation with his like to help
> Or solace his defects. No need that thou
> Should'st propagate, already infinite,
> And through all numbers absolute, though one;
> But man by number is to manifest
> His single imperfection, and beget
> Like of his like, his image multiplied,
> In unity defective, which requires
> Collateral love and dearest amity.
> Thou in thy secrecy although alone,
> Best with thyself accompanied, seek'st not
> Social communication . . .[19]

In unity defective. Could there be a better formulation of the tension in which Victor Frankenstein and his creature will be locked? The tension between the desire to enjoy one's own completeness and the fact that in the search for its satisfaction, this desire encounters the other, whose very existence means that the existence of the self can only be shared and incomplete. This impasse of the human condition had been emphasized by the seventeenth-century French moralists, no less than by Milton, albeit through another type of discourse. Enlightenment thought ignored and effaced it, or believed it had found the way out.

Although they were imbued with Enlightenment thought, Godwin, his daughter, and the poet Shelley (along with other early-nineteenth-century writers) illustrate this tension once more, *but through fictional narratives*. They thereby implicitly ratify the division which the Enlightenment set up – namely that, henceforth, a problematic of this nature no longer has a place in the domain of ideas. Thus, the narrative thread of *Caleb Williams* is obscure testimony to a truth which is at odds with the ideas that this novel is meant to defend and illustrate. This severance of thought from literature enables us to understand why the Romantic writers occupy an ambiguous and uneasy position in relation to academic philosophy.

Sometimes, in fact, they claim the sovereign freedom of fiction, and argue for art as a neutral terrain where responsibility need not be assumed for acts of protest (something, however, which their works appear to express). Thus Schiller, in his preface to *The Robbers*. Or Byron, in the preface to his *Cain* (1822), which is nonetheless a long philosophical poem on the problem of evil. *Cain*, says Byron, is a fiction, and the author does not share the ideas which he puts in the mouths of his characters. And 'If *Cain* can be "blasphemous", *Paradise Lost* is blasphemous,' he wrote to his publisher. This is Byron taking refuge behind the authority of the great poet in order to reduce the import of a justification of Lucifer which is, however, much more plainly affirmed in his *Cain* (where Lucifer fully deserves his name as bearer of light) than in *Paradise Lost*.[20]

Sometimes, instead, the Romantics see themselves as magi and prophets, or, in their own way, as philosophers. But the fact is that the author of a fictional narrative can hardly make a claim that his or her work expresses an important truth, for this could only be justified precisely by betraying the language of narration for the sake of borrowing the language of ideas. Thus, in his preface to *Frankenstein*, the poet Shelley presents it as a story which 'affords a point of view to the imagination for the delineating of human passions more comprehensive and commanding than any which the ordinary relations of existing events can yield'. But he neither develops nor justifies this claim (which I see as a very pertinent one). Likewise Chamisso, on his *Peter Schlemihl (The Man Who Lost His Shadow)*; like Shelley, Chamisso suggests that his narrative, *precisely because it is a fiction*, indicates a certain truth; but, not wishing to distort its nature, he refuses to translate this into the language of ideas. We could give a further example in Balzac who, beneath the title of *The Wild Ass's Skin*, tacks on *A Philosophical Novel*. Thus he declares a pretension, but without being able to do anything to justify it in the eyes of professional philosophers.

Let us say, in conclusion, that secular thought gives the narrative a very different place from the one it occupies within Christianity.

Within Christianity, the ideas are supported by the narrative – essentially that of the Fall and the Redemption. The ideas interpret the narrative – which, however, does not thereby become reabsorbed into the doctrine. The narrative, in fact, retains a power which is its own, since it is supposed to relate *what has taken place* prior to the present course of human life – what, *because it has taken place*, fundamentally determines its condition (when Milton wrote *Paradise Lost* – or, rather, dictated it to his daughters – for him it was not just a literary work referring to political events he had experienced; he was convinced that the events making up the narrative of his poem had really taken place, and were decisive for the human condition).

Since secular thought has its support in Reason, since it emancipates itself from the governance of dogma and of Revelation, either it does without the services of narrative or else, if it calls upon it, these narratives must show themselves to be permeable to reason. Thus, for example, narratives of the origin of political societies are told and taken seriously by philosophers – not because these narratives convey the highly valued history of what has taken place at the origin of epochs, but, rather, because they are rational speculations. When it comes to narratives which rebel against reason, or do not propose to illustrate ideas, they are quite free to go their own way, but on condition that they remain within the enclosure of literature; this word 'literature', with its aura of the modern values of Art and the Artist, thus discreetly fulfils the function of a *cordon sanitaire*.

7

Good Feeling

What we have noted so far allows us to illuminate one striking feature of the humanism that is current nowadays in the media and among certain intellectuals: its fondness for good feeling. A soothing ideology which attributes to human beings, on condition that they demonstrate an open mind and good will, the power to form harmonious and enriching relationships with anyone else, whatever the apparent differences between them. Under cover of rationalism, of 'trust in humanity' and 'messages of hope', good will is thus endowed with a power which, alas, experience shows to be overestimated.

As we have seen, this fine optimism was given a decisive impetus by Enlightenment thought. The virulence of human infinitude only expressed itself all the more freely within the register of narrative, but with any possibility of being heard in the world of ideas lost. In this chapter I would like to suggest that the rejection of an idea of human beings in which the bad infinite is granted a place has condemned the register of ideas to what one might call a puritanism of good feeling.

None the less, it would be wrong to believe that ideas are thereby sheltered from the tensions which run through fictional narratives; indeed, whatever we do, ideas are still worked out and experienced by flesh-and-blood creatures. This is why the puritanism of good feeling is not the result of some naive ignorance of these tensions but, rather, constitutes a measure of protection against them. Like a home in the midst of an inhospitable environment, good feeling offers us the relief of a more pleasant mental landscape than the real world in which humanity flounders.

Let us return for a moment to what we have learned from Mary Shelley's novel, for it is exactly tensions of the kind which *Frankenstein* dramatizes that simple-mindedness wishes to ignore. What is at issue in *Frankenstein* is being oneself fully and unconditionally. It is this radical desire which sets up a tension between two extremes: limitlessness and the need for other people – a tension which has the status of a duel, for it simultaneously requires the other and his destruction at one and the same time. It requires the other in a double sense: the other as an object, as a complement that will fulfil me; and the other thanks to whom I experience my own existence as real. This tension, simultaneously, requires the suppression of the other, for in a whole there is no room for two. To put it differently: once the other is required in order for me to fulfil my own existence, I depend on him in my very being; so the fact that he exists outside me and independently of me constitutes an intolerable obstacle to my full and total affirmation of myself.

How can we escape the pincers of these two antinomic yet inseparable requirements? We can, in simple terms, distinguish three main directions in which to seek (I do not say to find) a way out.

The first, as simple as it is brutal, consists in killing the other in order to be rid of him at last (unfortunately, as crime novels and ghost stories remind us, killing even a single person is an action with serious consequences; what is more, one cannot eliminate everyone).

The second consists in eliminating oneself – or, in a less extreme variant, keeping entirely to oneself. This is possibly an anticipation of the afterlife: the completeness found in God, not vainly sought in unsatisfactory relationships with others (but it is obviously not so easy to cut oneself off from this world).

If murder seems reprehensible and Salvation illusory, there remains a third way: clinging to an ideal made of idyllic relationships with others, and convincing oneself that – for one's own part, at least – one is prepared to 'accept the other'.

This last way seems more realistic than the first two. Like them, however, it claims to lead to the outcome of a genuine *solution*. Yet the problem as I have posed it allows of no solution; it is merely possible to *manage its tensions by means of compromise*. And this, moreover, is just how living in society helps us, in a very banal way, to avoid getting tangled up in the problem which concerns us here. In their best aspects, the practices of living in society protect us against our dream of achieving a genuine solution: in managing forms of compromise which are sufficiently viable, they allow us to renounce the realization in earnest of one or other of the radical solutions of which we dream. Living in society, with its attendant forms of civilization, for good or ill, maintains a *common world* between oneself and others, a world which simultaneously plays the part of a containment zone, a linkage, and a space where it is possible to attain a certain self-expansion and experience a sense of existing. If one is fortunate enough to find oneself sufficiently anchored in this common world, infinitude shifts into the background, its stranglehold slackens. We remain at odds with others, often severely, but in a way which is not destructive – or not too much so.

These observations will help us to understand how the violence of the tensions as well as the search for ideal or desperate solutions are not just expressed in *narratives* of fiction, but are secretly extended into the register of moral and rational *ideas*. These observations, in other words, will help us to understand *how the very negation of the tension or the apparent surmounting of it remain dependent upon it.*

Let us take one example. In Godwin's *Political Justice*, there is a short chapter on duelling.[1] The duel, he says, was first invented by barbarians for the gratification of revenge, and it was maintained as a received custom for the sake of upholding reputations. True courage, rather, lies in refusing the duel. How can one not subscribe to these reasonable notions? In *Caleb Williams*, Godwin again refers to the question of the duel. Squire Falkland has just been insulted and struck down in public by his envious rival. In this instance Godwin goes back to the thesis already formulated in *Political Justice*: agreeing to fight a duel constitutes a contemptible lack of self-love; refusing is not dishonourable, quite the opposite. And he adds: 'I can only be dishonoured by perpetrating an unjust action. My honour is in my own keeping, beyond the reach of all mankind.' Beneath the moral ideal can be glimpsed the narcissistic exaltation which fosters an illusion of omnipotence. Refusing the duel is yet another way of winning it, of enjoying one's own completeness by eliminating the other.

The ambiguity of this ideal position (a triumph of reason or a triumph of the passion for the self?) becomes even more obvious when the poet Shelley takes it up in *Prometheus Unbound*. Here, the confrontation is between Prometheus and Jupiter. Like Falkland in the episode I have just mentioned, like Caleb in the novel as a whole, Prometheus has been crushed, fettered by one stronger than himself. At the beginning of the poem he evokes the curse which he had formerly unleashed against the master of the universe, and predicts his imminent downfall. Will he then have his revenge on the oppressor? No, he will not even hate him any more, he will not even scorn him, he will pity him: 'Disdain! Ah no! I pity thee.' The duel, the first situation ('Fiend, I defy thee!') has been left behind – this, at any rate, is what Prometheus claims by displaying a moral sublimity which places him well above the god who keeps him in chains. It is clear enough, however, that this sublimity, far from constituting a return to moderation, extends and crowns the challenge launched by Prometheus. Similarly Caleb, fettered in a deep dungeon and observing that his master has now done his worst against him, represents the situation as turned to his advantage: ' "I exult," said I, "and reasonably, over the impotence of my persecutor".' Even in the depths of his sufferings, the bound Prometheus sees a force capable of counterbalancing Jupiter's omnipotence:

> I curse thee! Let a sufferer's curse
> Clasp thee, his torturer, like remorse;
> Till thine Infinity shall be
> A robe of envenomed agony;
> And thine Omnipotence a crown of pain.

For Godwin and for Shelley, this is a struggle against social injustice. But the desire for a more just society is mingled – and this probably goes for the Western world in general – with the desire to replace social bonds of interconnection with relationships of a moral nature. These would make it possible to cease being at odds with others, so that the triumph of the moral would resolve the antinomy which is the focus of this book (the impossibility of not depending on others, and the impossibility of reaching self-completeness through them).

The moral ideal embodied in Caleb or in Shelley's Prometheus seems a very long way from the rage which devours Frankenstein's creature. None the less, both positions have in common their boundlessness, which in the first case is masked and in the second manifest. By taking Rousseau as an example, we shall see how it is possible to move on from these two positions (the murderous hatred of the monster, the sublime independence of Caleb or Shelley's Prometheus) to a third, that of good feeling.

What is fascinating about Rousseau's work – at least to me – is not just that it is the product of a superior intelligence, but that running through it all is the antinomy which, in a different way, is expressed in *Frankenstein* and other narratives. The tension arising from this antinomy was to overwhelm Rousseau towards the end of his life, and would turn into a real nightmare for him. He was taken, he wrote at the time, 'for a monster', and he had become 'the horror of the human race' – so much so that 'an entire generation would of one accord take pleasure in burying me alive'.[2] It is probable that through his *Confessions* and his *Reveries* Rousseau transmitted to his disciple, Godwin, a good part of the energy that animated the latter's depiction of Caleb's misfortunes: 'Everything is finished for me on this earth,' Rousseau declares. 'Neither good nor evil can be done to me by any man. I have nothing left in the world to fear or hope for, and this leaves me in peace at the bottom of the abyss, a poor unfortunate mortal, but as unmoved as God himself.'[3]

Why this nightmare atmosphere (which is poorly disguised by the claim of sublimity with which the quoted passage ends)? Above, I distinguished between a *solution* to the antinomy and a *compromise* (or *management*). Rousseau rejects compromises, he has to have a solution: 'In the matter of happiness and enjoyment, I must have all or nothing.'[4] This, for example, is why, for Rousseau, mastur-bation comes closer to the all than to the nothing; with an imagin-ary partner one need not ask for consent or endure rejection.[5] Moreover, even when a woman he loved returned Rousseau's affection – even in this case, he wrote, he felt 'a feeling of oppres-sion'; because 'the mere idea that I was not all in all to her, caused her to seem hardly anything to me'.[6] A few lines earlier, Rousseau declares that he had always conducted himself in such a way as 'to prevent anyone being able to say to me with truth, in time of my misfortune: "You have well deserved it" '.[7] Certainly, it was not by his own choosing that he deemed as hardly anything someone for whom he was not everything, but that did not stop the victim of such a reaction from perceiving it as a mixture of tyrannical need and ingratitude. The thirst for completeness that Rousseau bore within him distilled, as he so aptly noted, its own poison, which prevented him from enjoying life: 'No, nature did not make me for enjoyment. It put into my bad head the poisoning of this ineffable happiness.'

We all have a share in this thirst for completeness; only, as a rule, the course of life leads us to put some water in our wine. Rousseau either cannot or does not want to do so. After his *Discourse on the Sciences and the Arts*, he takes up a position against the benevolent wisdom of the century, and finally professes a 'total renunciation of the world'.[8] Rousseau is not one of those accommodating theists whose like he has encountered among the *philosophes*. At heart he has remained a Calvinist (or, let us say, an Augustinian): being subject to the scrutiny of himself alone – or, what comes down to the same thing, the scrutiny of God alone – suits him, confirms him in his 'all or nothing', and turns a value of the second order into an anchorage in a common social world. This, as has often been observed, is what the ageing Rousseau says about his reformed life and his solitude, his unique personality and his superior morality. But there is also – the *Confessions* repeatedly testify to this – his tendency to discourage the kindness shown to him by those around him, and his extraordinary propensity to undermine these acts of kindness, so that they fail. Repaying them with his gratitude would represent too heavy a tribute for Rousseau. Likewise, he prefers to turn his back on his success as a writer (a success, however, that was both rapid and resounding) rather than recognize that he owes this gratification to his readers.

It is for this same reason that his conscience fails to trouble him on the very points I have just mentioned. A famous passage in *Émile* tells us how Rousseau thought of moral consciousness: as a 'divine instinct', an 'immortal and heavenly voice'. (It strikes me, more modestly, that our 'moral consciousness' corresponds, rather, to the feeling that one must personally strive for the maintenance of everything which brings about a certain coexistence, a state from which one benefits and to which, consequently, one owes something.) Rousseau remains faithful to the Christian idea which Kant was to theorize: moral consciousness is interior and transcendent; as a result, paradoxically, it owes nothing to others. It is therefore not surprising that this consciousness, which in Rousseau is secretly animated by a narcissistic desire for the absolute, should spare him the reproaches which his blind spot would indeed deserve. Likewise, scrupulous though it may be, this consciousness does not allow him to suspect the sad truth: that the persecutions he suffers – both real and imaginary – are partly the backlash of his own desire to rid himself of others, and that, as a result, the sense of guilt he feels is not inappropriate: he really is guilty. Not guilty of some misdeed, but guilty of the desire in whose grip he is held, despite himself.

It would take a whole book to show, first, how Rousseau's narratives (the *Confessions*, the *Reveries*, *La Nouvelle Héloïse*) testify to the tension which both stimulates and oppresses him; and secondly, how this tension runs through his theoretical works, and how Rousseau made the most of it with genius, racked as he was by the desire to find a solution to the insoluble, and to work out how one can be both all to oneself and in seamless harmony with others (not de-completed, not alienated by the bonds which attach us or chain us to them).

In the effort of his thought, Rousseau simultaneously follows and resists his inclination. He is strongly tempted by the idealization of an original state (hence those formulations to which his ideas have often been reduced: 'man is born good, it is society which depraves him'; 'man is born free and everywhere is in chains'). Nevertheless, he admits, man can only truly be man and develop his faculties in the company of his fellows.[9] The main business for Rousseau is working out how, against the grain of the existing social contract which dooms human beings to incompleteness, they have come to know or could know a state of completeness, where the self and the Whole coincide.

To connect human beings to completeness through the touch-stone of an original state (followed by a fall) is to ask the question: how did we reach the point where we are now? (*Discourse on the Origin and Basis of Inequality*). Connecting them to completeness by means of a theory of education is to ask the question: by which manner of education can 'natural man' be preserved? (*Émile*). Connecting them to completeness through a political theory: how is man to be denatured in such a way that he can identify with the entire body politic without thereby being subordinated to anyone? (*The Social Contract*).

For all that Rousseau did his best to take his fellows as they are, he did not manage it (on this point, to be frank, it is hard to take him to task): he loves them, but on condition that they remain imaginary (this is the case for Julie, the heroine of *La Nouvelle Héloïse*, or the virtuous and frugal inhabitants of Le Valais, whom he knows only from afar and whom he idealizes). Loving at a distance, loving through some interposed representation,[10] in the belief that one genuinely loves; this is one of the illusions main-tained by good feeling, one which consoles us a little for the commonplace discords to which daily life exposes us (for example, in the experience of work relationships, of married life or condo-minium meetings).

Simple-mindedness, when all is said and done, is fuelled by two things. One of these is a permanent temptation: the need to idealize, to furnish one's mental landscape with flattering and comforting scenes, while concentrating evil in a circumscribed area of the world which is external to and distant from oneself. The other derives from a specific idea about human beings, an idea based on the conviction that they should be able to fulfil themselves in a full and thorough manner – that is to say, on the basis of a *solution*, not just through *management*. This is why it is worth the trouble of asking oneself what prevents Rousseau (or what prevents *us*) from imagining that *management* could be preferable to a *solution*. For Rousseau to have removed this impediment, he would have needed to recognize the ambivalence of his own fount of infinitude; to admit, consequently, that completeness has its bad side; to stop idealizing his requirement of all or nothing; and thus allow himself the right to feel bad feelings (feelings and desires which are, in any case, no worse in him than in each one of us).

Obviously, people did not wait for Rousseau to come along in order to cast evil outside themselves and take up the puritanism of good feeling. But Rousseau can nevertheless be regarded as one of the patron saints of contemporary simple-mindedness (even if the first prize ought to go to others before him – Hutcheson, for instance[11]). This simple-mindedness has certain specific features in Rousseau (like the one exemplified by calling Madame de Warens 'Mamma', or his tendency to regard himself as a victim). But in him these singularities were in accord with the spirit of the time that exempted man from the inner source of wickedness and transferred it onto the external world (which had the prime effect, precisely, of upgrading on a grand scale the valued status of the total, therefore ideally good, victim – a status hitherto reserved for the crucified Almighty). The adoption of this vision of the world by enlightened minds is probably inseparable from the movement towards the secularization of ideas and the progress of positivist knowledge. At the same time, however, it marks a decisive stage in what one might call the process of trivializing the infinite. This process had taken a significant step with the development of monotheism and a rational metaphysics, a development which relegated to the realm of fiction the idea that the world, in order to become habitable, had to wrench itself out of chaos and turn this chaos to its advantage – a chaos which offered a limitless fount of resources, but also a chaos made destructive by its very lack of limits. With Enlightenment thought, it is not just the original source of human beings which, in the person of the one and only God, becomes reduced to a benign infinity, it is also the bad inner infinity from which, from then on, we are delivered.

Thanks to the utilitarian and rational conception of *Homo economicus*, individuals renounce the infinitude of their self-love in order to limit themselves to serving their interests. And thanks to a secularized Christianity (primarily through Rousseau and Kant), despite everything they maintain a link to the infinite, in the blander but highly commendable form of their moral consciousness. On the one hand this means a reasonable acceptance of a reduced self-image (having a horizon bounded by profit and social success). On the other, it is still necessary to keep some way of escaping from one's own mediocrity, and of self-idealization. One kind of temptation lies in a rediscovery of the grandeurs of manly heroism, but the opportunity for yielding to this remains connected only to exceptional situations (the conqueror in battle, or else the resistance fighter, or the revolutionary militant). So all that is left within our reach, in the ordinary life that is ours, is this form of self-idealization which consists in the puritanism of good feeling (holding forth about doing good, sympathizing with victims, expressing indignation about the wickedness of others).

Subscribing to this *purified* representation of the self offered nowadays by the rational subject (the subject of knowledge) amounts to the extension of an old dualism which has assumed new forms. Thus, since fictional narratives draw their energy from a non-dualist source, rational thought takes up its abode under a regime which is in contradiction with theirs. But it is a contradiction which remains invisible, and therefore unthinkable, so long as ideas and narratives are regarded as two heterogeneous registers which have no common yardstick.

If this separation did not prevent reason (in the guise of German Romantic philosophy) from aiming to recuperate myth, it forced it into misrecognition. There is no better indication of the depth of the misunderstanding than this passage from Friedrich Schlegel: 'Supreme beauty, and indeed supreme order, are only ever those of Chaos, which is to say of a Chaos which only awaits the touch of love to be arrayed within a world of harmony, of a Chaos akin to mythology and ancient poetry.'[12]

The *muthos* of the Ancient Greeks and other polytheistic civilizations certainly does not present harmony as being in continuity with Chaos (this is the opposite of the modern Promethean spirit, which has fondly imagined that harmony could come out of Chaos). Within the logic of a polytheistic narrative like Hesiod's *Theogony*, for example, it is true that what is constructive makes use of what is destructive, but at a very high cost: the cost of divisions and distancing – that is to say, *the cost of a loss of completeness.* The Romantic conception of mythology is applied to idealized myths; it misrecognizes the internal logic of the myths which it aims to revive; similarly, it misrecognizes those powerful narratives – like *Frankenstein* – which Romanticism itself has given us. In the narratives, ideal, idyllic completeness is only a limited limitlessness, for the narrative, unlike the philosophy, does not forget that beyond idyllic completeness there is always the bad infinite. This could be shown even in relation to a story as God-fearing as *Paul et Virginie.* For the sake of holding his readers' attention, Bernard de Saint-Pierre thought it best to add to his depiction of good feeling another of irreparable disaster, a shipwreck; for without the destructive power of the ocean, the Edenic idyll of the young lovers could not have achieved that intensity which can come only from a boundless lack of limits. Likewise, the reader of Shelley's *Prometheus* might well believe that his compelling interest is prompted by an ideal of justice, but he derives just as much pleasure – albeit obscurely – from a character whose self-affirmation recognizes no bounds.

8

Idyllic Completeness, Violent Completeness: The Ambiguity of the Desire for Reparation

To shake the torpor of good feeling in which current thinking wallows, we need to go all the way back to the fundamental and insoluble tension which it helps us to forget. In this chapter, I would like to show:

- how our desire to escape from this tension propels our dreams and our behaviour in two directions: that of 'sweet completeness' (concord, idyll and paradise), and that of 'violent completeness' (being *one* in destruction);
- how these two orientations tend to be combined and confused within us.

By depicting himself as the victim of unjust persecution, Rousseau presents himself as good and worthy of compassion. In Chapter 5 ('Pity for the Monster'), we saw the monster adopt the same line of argument, the same posture, as Rousseau. And it had appeared that while it inspired a feeling of pity in readers, the monster also offered them the pleasure of a figure of omnipotence. Unlike Rousseau, however, when the monster tells the story of its life, it does not entirely lose sight of the destructive feelings in which it is enmeshed. In the picture she draws of the idyllic and edifying little society observed day after day by the monster, Mary Shelley appears to be following the same path to good feeling already outlined in *La nouvelle Héloïse* (together with Shelley and Byron, during their

famous sojourn in Switzerland, she was able to contemplate the
landscapes Rousseau describes in his novel). Thus she invites the
reader to share in the pleasures of sweet completeness – pleasures
with which pastoral poetry had lulled generations of readers before
her. But she has read Milton (who also took up residence on the
shores of Lake Leman, in the same villa which Byron rented and in
which he had numerous conversations with the Shelleys), and she
makes the monster read Milton. Sweet completeness did not make
her forget how much stronger was the inclination for a violent and
exclusive completeness. 'Many times I considered Satan as the fitter
emblem of my condition; for often, like him, when I viewed the
bliss of my protectors, the bitter gall of envy rose within me,' says
the monster. Victor Frankenstein, too, in his own envy of God's
creative power, likewise compares himself to Satan: 'like the arch-
angel who aspired to omnipotence, I am chained in an eternal
hell'.

Earlier, Milton had shown Satan spying on Adam and Eve. The
couple at the dawn of time present an ideal and flower-decked
picture which owes more to the pastoral tradition than to any
biblical austerity. Satan, too, is almost seduced by the charming
couple ('whom my thoughts pursue/With wonder, and could love),
and Eve, 'with nymph-like step fair virgin pass', disarms him.

> . . . aside the devil turned
> For envy, yet with jealous leer malign
> Eyed them askance, and to himself thus plained:
> 'Sight hateful, sight tormenting! Thus these two,
> Imparadised in one another's arms,
> The happier Eden, shall enjoy their fill
> Of bliss on bliss, while I to hell am thrust,
> Where neither joy nor love, but fierce desire,
> Among our other torments not the least,
> Still unfulfilled, with pain of longing pines.

This longing which eats up the heart of the envious one (but on
which he simultaneously feeds) is a longing, not for the taste of

pleasure, '. . . but all pleasure to destroy,/Save what is in destroying; other joy/ To me is lost.'[1]

William Blake's famous opinion, in *The Marriage of Heaven and Hell*, that Milton was 'of the Devil's party without knowing it' is still repeated; this has a tendency to turn the poet into a herald of the modern spirit of revolt. No doubt Milton's political progressivism justifies this interpretation. None the less, it should not allow us to forget the deep Augustinianism which Milton shared with many other thinkers of his time, be they Puritan humanists or Jansenists. As well as *The City of God* (whose Book XXII had supplied the subject of *Paradise Lost*), Milton certainly knew the striking descriptions of envious longing which Saint Augustine offers at the beginning of the *Confessions*. Augustine imagines himself as a baby desiring the breast with evil avidity. 'I have watched and experienced for myself the jealousy of a small child: he could not even speak, yet he glared with livid fury at his fellow nursling.' Augustine also stresses the impotence of the infant he once was: when those around him did not become slaves to his unexpressed wishes, he writes, 'I would throw a tantrum . . . I would take revenge on them by bursting into tears.'[2] Augustine had understood what Enlightenment thought has made us forget: *another need not have injured us for us to desire reparation from him*: the dizzying gap between our awareness of ourselves and the limited place we occupy among others is enough to make us hate them. From this point of view, Milton's Satan deploys, radicalizes and even, so to speak, theorizes the Augustinian vision of human malignity.

In an explicit and determined way, Satan has devoted himself to the disastrous completeness of the bad infinite, while simultaneously rejecting the idealized coexistence which is sweet completeness:

> His trust was with the eternal to be deemed
> Equal in strength, and rather than be less
> Cared not to be at all; with that care lost
> Went all his fear: of God, or hell, or worse.[3]

As René Girard rightly put it (in relation to the protagonists of Camus's *The Outsider*, it must be admitted): 'basing the whole of existence on this void that one carries inside oneself means transforming powerlessness into all-powerfulness, it means enlarging the desert island within to the scale of infinity'.[4]

In effect, Satan moves through an infinite kingdom. Here he is, for example, contemplating

> The secrets of the hoary deep – a dark
> Illimitable ocean without bound,
> Without dimension; where length, breadth, and height,
> And time and place, are lost; where eldest Night
> And Chaos, ancestors of nature, hold
> Eternal anarchy, amidst the noise
> Of endless wars, and by confusion stand.

Satan, says Milton, carries Hell within himself; but the poet never confuses Hell and Chaos. Satan's inner hell is only the consequence of his identification with Chaos. Nothing can compare with him but the destructive sublimity of

> . . . the vast immeasurable abyss,
> Outrageous as a sea, dark, wasteful, wild,
> Up from the bottom turned by furious winds
> And surging waves, as mountains to assault
> Heaven's height, and with the centre mix the pole.[5]

Chaos is the space of the poem; it is what gives the figure of Satan his great breadth. The Christian tradition alone would not have been enough for Milton to have forged this extraordinary character: he needed the inspiration of paganism – of the Titans and the Chaos depicted in Hesiod's *Theogony*. As a consequence, Milton comes close to heresy: the God of *Paradise Lost* did not create the world *ex nihilo*, but out of Chaos. When Milton writes of 'The rising world of waters dark and deep,/Won from the void and formless infinite', one might believe he is thinking of the idea of infinite space which he perhaps discussed with Galileo when he visited him in his prison at Fiesole.[6] But when the poet refers to 'uncreated night', when he writes that upon the first word uttered by God '. . . the formless mass,/This world's material mould, came to a heap:/Confusion heard his voice, and wild uproar/Stood ruled, stood vast infinitude confined'; when he states; 'As yet this world was not, and Chaos wild/Reigned where these heavens now roll, where earth/now rests',[7] it becomes clear that Milton is skirting the Christian dogma of a God who created the world out of nothing (nothing other than Himself) for the sake of the pagan conception of an unformed Chaos pre-existing the differentiated world (a more or less universal conception anyway). This hardly orthodox vision enables Milton to make Satan much more than an agent of evil whose powers remain under the control of a God who alone is truly infinite: in his Satan he can deploy a whole aspect of human subjectivity. Satan is a person like us and, like us, he is racked by infinitude. A person whose interior space exceeds the dimensions of Being and reaches those of Non-Being, of the omnipotence of Chaos (in a sense Non-being is more than Being, since everything which is exists at the cost of differences and limits, while Nothingness is limitless).

Thus, Milton's vast poem sets at the core of the human soul this vertiginous well of which Satan becomes the emblem and the mirror. Before our very eyes Milton casts the bad infinite, and refuses to say that it is nothing, and that when all is said and done, only the good infinite exists. This is not to say that he was on the side of Satan but, rather, that he was not on the side of the *philosophes* (since they cling to more benign forms of the desire for completeness). In Milton's day, philosophy set up a kind of rivalry with the Creator, but a licit rivalry: what counted was not to *exist* in His place, only to *know* by putting oneself in His place. Reason, which human beings share with God, enables the philosopher to think what God thought when he created the world. Thus, when Leibniz set out to prove that there could be no vacuum in the universe, and supported this with the thoughts which the Creator, in his view, must have had, even his adversaries took him seriously, and continued to argue with him. Milton's great superiority over the *philosophes* who devised systems was that he had not watered

down the desire for more-being by restricting it to the desire for
global Knowledge. For his Satan, being is something quite different
from knowing; this is why Satan would never be able to find any
certainty of existing, any foundation for the self, in the *cogito*.

Descartes, in his own way, competes with this mirage, with that
supreme reflection of himself which he names God. In one sense,
the *cogito* allows him to win the day; in another sense, on the
contrary, he assuages this rivalry. The certainty of thinking brings
with it the certainty of having self-consciousness; and Descartes
seems to take it for granted that the fact of being self-conscious is
equivalent to the fact of being, as he says, a *substance*, that is to say,
a stable substratum, something which *is* – an abusive identification
whose importance has been rightly underlined by Giorgio Agamben.[8] This equivalence enables the 'thinking substance' to appropriate a power of being-in-itself which is an attribute of God (an
attribute which is added or takes over from to the immortal soul
with which Christianity had already endowed it). But at the same
time, since the fact of existing as a thinking subject (a subject of
knowledge) allows the subject to enjoy his or her completeness on
the basis of the *idea* of infinity, and since this idea has its source in
God, there is room for two. In the case of Milton's character, this
harmony between limitlessness and coexistence is unviable. That
there might be something of the infinite in the fact of having self-
consciousness does not pacify Satan (from this point of view, he is
more like each one of us than the Cartesian subject) because Satan,
for his part, does not confuse consciousness and substance: he is,
much rather, consciousness of nonexistence. For him, thinking of
the infinite is not being infinite, and the idea of the all is not the
all. The divine attribute which Satan longs to appropriate is therefore not omniscience, it is existence itself. But, as Milton says
through Adam – the perfection of being-all, of being-one, is inac-
cessible to men, who cannot but be multiple. There is therefore no
solution, except self-destruction in reigning over the limitlessness
of one's own nothingness: 'better to reign in Hell than serve in
Heaven!'

Whatever happiness one human being might bring to another,
and however enviable the sweet completeness of Adam and Eve

'imparadised in one another's arms', an idyllic existence is never total, since it presupposes a division and an acceptance of otherness: each one is indebted to the other, and both are indebted to the surrounding environment in which and thanks to which they live. The figure of Satan reminds us that the subterranean part of the human soul is haunted by the radical rejection of otherness, and is not disposed to make do with happiness.

As an escape from the constraints, the wear and tear and the sufferings of everyday life, we dream of the good things, but also of the bad things that would deliver us from them – of a paradise, but also of a destruction. And in merging, these two dreams make us prisoners of their confusion. These observations may well strike the reader as abstract. I am going to illustrate them with the example of some human events in which are mingled the desire to *escape to infinitude* (in order to rediscover peace and harmony) and the desire *to abandon oneself to it* (in order to enjoy limitlessness).

At the beginning of this book, I gave an example of those irrational terrors to which children are subject, oscillating, as between day and night, between the bounded and reassuring world they share with others and a solitary and suffocating encounter with omnipotence. For most of us, as we move from childhood to adulthood, the experience of terror alters progressively into a feeling, which is usually also short-lived, of depressing emptiness (the link between these two types of experience being constituted by anxiety). Alcohol or other drugs are almost universally employed to relieve anxiety and fill up the emptiness. The first few glasses produce a haze, a mellowness, a pleasant fuzziness. At the same time, they soften what is awkward and distant in relationships with others. This is the peace – not to say euphoria – which takes the edge off uncomfortable self-confrontations, as well as the arduous and restricting side of dealing with others. A fullness in place of the emptiness, floating in the ocean instead of struggling over barren terrain strewn with jagged rocks. And then, the more you drink, the more hell invades Eden.[9] Either other people almost cease to exist, and you are foundering alone in what has become a swamp (rather like the consul in *Under the Volcano*), or your feeling of being unfettered, together with the affirmation of an otherwise insecure

or humiliated manliness, offers a way out of accumulated resentments; then, instead of the relief of finding well-being with others,
relief comes from taking it out on them with aggression.

Alcohol, late at night, can lead to domestic rows. These, as we
saw in relation to Victor Frankenstein's confrontation with his
creature on Mont Blanc, reveal the same mixture of contrary
desires. A search for relief which swings between the dream of
fusion and the wish to murder. In an overwhelming state of anxiety
and distress, for the sake of love, for the sake of what the other
owes us, we require of her or him an adequate remedy for the
vertiginous deficit of existence which we feel. The other is simultaneously the one we call to for help and the one we rage against as
being responsible for our own distress. This other, also made
anxious by the weight of these demands, feels embattled and
powerless, with the resulting impulse either to shut us out or to
retaliate.

But, just as there are ways of drinking that go together with
sociability, there are also socially acceptable ways of getting one's
own back on others for the agonies we suffer because of the gap
between infinitude and our paucity of being. War, obviously, and
other kinds of struggle or competition. By forging bonds between
those who fight side by side, for each individual, war or struggle
fashions an area of self-expansion which goes far beyond what a
state of peace can achieve; in addition to the first source of self-
expansion which the fighter discovers in the solidarity which joins
him to his comrades, there is also the fact of destroying the
boundaries which others – adversaries this time – set up against the
expansion of one's being.

Here we encounter the wider question of 'them' and 'us' – two
groups set against one another by class hatred, racial hatred,
religious hatred, or any other form of divisiveness. Such hatreds can
seem utterly deplorable, and the outside observer is often surprised
that the two groups expend so much energy in activities which
make their lives difficult and are quite clearly against their own
interests. Nevertheless, as I have tried to show, once one imagines
issues of relationship not in terms of interest but in terms of a
feeling of existing, one can say that hating produces an immediate

extra-being which is hard to give up. What is profitable for the members of 'us' is not being approved by 'them', it is approval among themselves. For the members of 'us', belittling 'them' confirms the value of the features which draw them together and allow their mutual appreciation. Of course, it is the members of 'them' who foot the the bill for the operation (reimbursed by hating 'us'). But the disapproval or hatred which comes from 'them' is not enough to damage the 'us''s feeling of existing – precisely because 'them', by definition, is not a part of 'us'. It is likewise understandable that admonitions cut no ice with this 'us'; since moral discourse issues from a third authority; this authority is often perceived by 'us' as being one of 'them'. With this combination of conditions, 'us' can only persevere in its mode of being, and only an alteration in the balance of power can avert it from the road to disaster.

The exercise of power constitutes another form of compromise between the ideal of coexistence and that of maximum self-affirmation. The person upon whom others depend draws from them the extra-being which a lover might not necessarily receive from the person whom he or she loves, nor the fighter from the adversary; indeed, the person exercising acknowledged power avoids the risks of physical violence as well as the mortifications of unrequited love. Moreover, when one has power, one can take revenge. There is certainly gratification in extracting compensation from those who have wronged us. But taking revenge on those who have done nothing to us affords a kind of a supreme compensation, since it is unhindered by any law, even the law of an eye for an eye: it is the sovereign dream of someone who imagines himself as 'master of the world'. Nietzsche had understood this – or rather, he had *almost* understood it. For in setting up an opposition, as he did in *On the Genealogy of Morals*,[10] between slaves animated by resentment and, above them, noble men who derive from their own selves the idea of what is good and use their will to power like innocent big cats, Nietzsche projects on to reality his own desire to escape interdependence. If it were true that power really deemed as nothing those it crushes, it would derive its gratification from itself while crushing no one – which is unheard of. Ignoring someone is yet another way of deriving gratification from him; it therefore means needing him, even if the one who ignores likes to believe that his attitude comes from a sovereign independence. And however overriding it might consider itself, the feeling of self-worth can be exerted only within a context of comparison. The pure will to power – that is to say, an expansion of the self liberated from the desire to exist in the mind of others – does not exist. There is no escape from the wish to feel valued, and what defines a value, of any kind, is that one is not alone in appreciating it. Vincent Descombes notes the difficulty in Deleuze's book on Nietzsche: in order to feel incomparably valuable, one has to compare oneself, and therefore not be incomparable.[11]

Here is another example, on a more modest scale, of activities which partake of the same logic (which is not, I stress, a logic of ideas, but a logic of existence, an 'economy' of existence): political discussions between friends, colleagues or relatives. This type of exchange, as we know, can easily turn into a free-for-all, or else – when there is a male particularly keen to emphasize his pre-eminence – a vehement monologue. For anyone who embarks on a political diatribe, the issues at stake in what is said, consciously or otherwise, are not *just* of a political nature. Talking about political problems means talking about what is going wrong on a massive scale – about a fundamental ill or its remedy. In 'who is to blame', 'what is to blame', oneself and one's relations with others thus become obscurely involved. But at the same time, talking politics is a response to the wish to show that one is discerning, to show one's interlocutors that one is in a position to survey the general movement of society.[12] The global nature of this horizon and the scope of the issues tend to arouse desires of infantile omnipotence; these combine with unhealed wounds to self-esteem; this underlying twin current then begins to resonate within the explicit content of the discussion and, imperceptibly, interferes in it. One wants things to improve. Disasters, outbreaks of violence, human selfishness, lack of foresight, injustice – the whole human race a prey to discords and discordances of all kinds. One would like these things to be sorted out, one would like them to end, one would like a solution – in other words, peace and harmony. But discord is others – the plurality of people, groups, ways of being, interests, classes, nations. Therefore one clashes with others just as one comes up against the wall of one's own powerlessness. As a result, the quest for an order that will do good, for a remedy that is in everyone's interest, ends up becoming confused with a rejection of otherness, and with the desire to eliminate it. And in the very act of speaking, one asserts oneself and, throughout one's speech, one occupies the throne of the powerful of the earth. One's gaze sweeps across a vast theatre in which one's interlocutors are reduced to the role of mute and nonexistent spectators.

This limitlessness, when it is topped up with too much alcohol or a depressed mood, all too quickly turns against the one who is intoxicated by it. He has taken upon himself the ills of the country and the evils of the world, and these become too heavy a burden, so nothing will come of it. Here he is, dragged in, overwhelmed by a tide of disasters in which, because of the good feeling upon which he prides himself, he is unable to recognize his own harmful infinitude projected on to the outside world. Reading the newspaper sometimes triggers an analogous inclination. 'There's no doubt about it, things are going from bad to worse.' We deplore it. But at the same time, since what goes badly tends towards the infinite, while what goes well tends only towards mediocrity, despite ourselves we are sucked into the sight of catastrophe, and we unknowingly enjoy what sustains our darker thoughts.

On an even more everyday level, there are those words which people say to one another all the time in the thousands of staff canteens and restaurants across the world. Things aren't going as they should, it's annoying, it's tedious; other people (those who are placed higher in the hierarchy, those who are lower, those who belong to *another* department) are not doing what they ought to be doing. As compensation for the lack of harmony which limits the expansion of our being, we treat ourselves to the pleasure of feeling superior to those whom we criticize; and thus we fuel the discord of which we complain.

The ambivalence which underlies political discussions (the quest for the general good, the enjoyment of a discourse of domination) is to be found just as much in the realm of religion.

Let us pause for a moment over one example: human sacrifice as practised by the Aztecs. The movement of the world consumes energy and, as the Aztecs saw it, the radiance of the sun presented the best proof of this cosmic expenditure. Taking into account the world as a whole, the breakdown of time into its major cycles thereby leads on to perspectives of chaos. What if the orderly course of the world were to slacken at a point marking the end of a cycle, and be unable to start up again! What if the sun, eaten up by an eclipse, were to be extinguished! What if, under cover of darkness, ghosts were to invade the cities and devour the inhabitants! It is therefore most important to renew the energy of the sun which reigns over this economy of disaster; this means that it must be given the richest and most energizing food, the blood of warriors captured in battle.[13] In his fascinating study of Aztec sacrifice, Christian Duverger puts forward the idea of a possible draining of cosmic energy as being an intuition of what nowadays we call entropy. Having taken this hypothesis as a guiding principle, he finds it 'odd' that among the Aztecs entropy 'is largely expressed through the *oral* function: the sun must *eat* those sacrificed in order to be nourished'; and that its emblems are the eagle and the jaguar, Mexico's two greatest predators.[14] Likewise he presents as a paradox the fact that human sacrifice, whose principle is justified by the economic necessity of sustaining the sun's energy, 'leads in practice to a prodigious consumption of wealth'; he observes that 'sacrifice is an abyss' (countless captives sacrificed in the course of festivities worthy of Hollywood mega-productions, wars of conquest waged further and further away in order to direct fresh resources to increasingly grandiose sacrificial monuments[15]).

In these observations, the interpretation of Aztec sacrifice comes up against an obstacle which strikes me as being linked to the use made by the author of the idea of economy. Economy in Christian Duverger's terms – rather like Bataille's 'general economy' as formulated in *La Part maudite* – is applied to a collection of events much wider than what Adam Smith, Marx or Keynes meant by economy. And accordingly, the description of an economy involving not just the management of material wealth but also that of the power exercised over the Aztec populations and those around them, as well as the articulation of social energy with that of the universe, becomes a description of great interest – one that is, moreover, more precise than Bataille's speculations, which are quite evocative enough. It is nevertheless a fact that, in order to go beyond the assumptions that the classical economy has handed down to us, we need to do more than broaden its field to non–commercial and non-utilitarian practices, or invert its principles (by shifting from *profit* to *expenditure*). It is equally necessary to deconstruct the conception of human beings which the economic sciences have held to be evident and universal. It is within this perspective that I would like to underline the incidence of the bad infinite here.

If the Aztecs saw the sun as an insatiable devourer endlessly blackmailing them, this was certainly not just because of their intuition of how things run down. It was also because, quite simply, they liked the idea. And in this respect, they are like the majority of other societies which are fond of telling themselves stories in which human beings have to grapple with ogres, vampires, ghouls, cyclopses, werewolves, panthers, tigers or other man-eating creatures. Only, in tales about ogres, it is usually a matter of avoiding these bloodthirsty attentions rather than responding to them. Tom Thumb, like so many other characters in European, African or Asian tales, arises from a different realm than that of the ogre, using resources linked not to limitlessness but instead to limitation, to the play of differences, to the currency of speech, to references within social space. The ogre story that the Aztecs told themselves, and whose dramatization was organized by the central authority in Mexico, gave more room to infinitude. The Aztecs saw clearly the need to limit the destructive threat of the bad infinite in order to maintain a differentiated and habitable world. At the same time, however, they could not resist the seduction exerted over them by the image of an all-absorbing power. By placing themselves under the threat of a devourer whom they could pacify only by yielding to its voracity, *they joined the struggle against Chaos to the pleasure of plunging into it.* Thus, while contributing to the world's order, they imitated the predator from which they sought to protect themselves; like it, they carried out the slaughter of human prey and turned to anthropophagy.

A comparable compromise underlies a type of human sacrifice which at first sight is very different: the type still practised in nineteenth-century India by the 'Thugs'.[16] Our rationalism might lead us to regard the Thugs as a simple brotherhood of thieves. But in reality it was just as important for them to kill as to steal, and they always used the same method, strangulation. Like the Aztecs, they justified their crimes in the name of the threat hanging over humanity from an omnipotent destructive power. In their view, murder was a sacrifice – that is to say, an evil from which springs a greater good. By immolating a certain number of human beings to the goddess Kali, they kept her appetite for destruction within tolerable bounds; if they had abstained from doing so, death would instead have struck down a huge mass of people.

It was not the sun or Kali that the Aztecs and the Thugs were really dealing with, but their own infinitude. To ward it off, to limit its pressure, they paid it a tribute. Whatever benefit one might find in living in material and psychic worlds that are differentiated, ordered and bounded, one never entirely renounces limitlessness and the desire for omnipotence. Moreover, in the instances I have just cited, the need to struggle against Chaos, far from being expressed in the building of some fundamental barrier capable of resisting it, is presented as the need to confront it, to enter into a relation with it in order to counter it with a remedy comparable with the evil, a means of pacification which responds to its voracity. And since only the infinite can be measured against the infinite, the remedy ultimately fosters the evil.

Anyone who is absorbed by the desire to make good, to save someone who is beloved, engages in an analogous 'economy' (a logic of existence). Why does he persist in staring into the bottomless well which the other asks him to fill up? Because in this well, and only in it, does he find the image of his own completeness, of the All which he has to be in order to give the other the All that he or she lacks. Thus, the more he makes good, the more he becomes embroiled in the irreparable.

It is customary to counter the polytheistic religions, which are regarded as barbaric to one degree or another, with the moral shift which inscribed its necessity at the heart of Jewish – and later

Christian – monotheism. This is what Lessing does, for example, when he retraces the history of human progress; vindicating the Enlightenment and the Masonic movement, Lessing situates poly-theism on the side of ideology and darkness, and the coming of a single God on the side of reason and progress.[17] This view is partly made up of truth, but also partly of prejudice, as I underlined in Chapter 1 ('The Price of Monotheism'). Here I would like to refer more precisely to the way in which Christianity associates an ideal of justice and harmony between men with an ideal which tends towards the infinite.

The Son of God was made flesh and offered himself up as a sacrifice for our salvation; this is the essential tenet of Christian doctrine. The story of the incarnation, which begins with the joy of Christmas and culminates in the tragedy of the calvary suffered by Christ, upholds the evangelical message of humanity. But there is also another side of the doctrine to which Christ's passion gives all its weight: how can we close the infinite distance which separates man from God? Only the infinite can redeem the infinite. Only the long and ignominious agony endured by a God constitutes an adequate oblation to redeem the original sin which condemned men to their mortal state.

Christ is certainly very different from the sun-ogre of the Aztecs: far from preying vampire-like upon humanity, he offers himself up to it instead through the Eucharist, like the pelican feeding its children from its own flesh. However, the blood shed by the Man-God (Pascal points this out, and all of Christian preaching empha-sizes it) does not in any way lighten the weight upon each one of us of an *infinite debt*: after all that Jesus suffered for you, you will never do enough to be worthy of the immortality He gives to you.

For the Christian, the mystery of the Incarnation therefore binds together in the closest possible way two obligations which in them-selves are very different: to love one's neighbour, and to ensure his salvation. A message of humanity is thus blended with a message of inhumanity; images of goodness with pictures of Apocalypse. Since charity and eternal life are linked, suffering bears an ambiguous status within Christianity. Suffering is an evil; it must be relieved. One must, like the Good Samaritan, extend a helping hand to the wretched of the earth; one must struggle against injustice and violence. But suffering also means the Passion of Christ, who consecrated its value by marking it with the seal of the infinite. Jesus at Gethsemane, alone in the night; Jesus overwhelmed by his foreknowledge of the calvary which awaits him; Jesus addressing a desperate prayer to his Father, and nevertheless accepting his fate. This Jesus recalls Job, likewise solitary, and finding at last, in the depths of the abjection in which he is cast down, a face-to-face encounter with true and infinite grandeur. Here pain is presented as a mirror of completeness, as what comes closest to it, as something which can be transmuted into actual completeness simply by a mere reversal. It is therefore a matter of accepting this pain, approaching it, and of self-mortification through contact with wretchedness. Here we have all the ambiguity of kissing the leper or of Mother Teresa's refuge, all the ambiguity of 'the spirit of sacrifice'.

The Christian's relationship to suffering swings in two directions (these are opposing only from an outside point of view, since for the Christian they converge and merge). The first of these aims at *improvement*. It is expressed through actions with practical effects (this is the axis of social Christianity). The second aims at *reversal*. It is expressed through a logic of sacrifice which is animated by the expectation of redemption; it is therefore inscribed within an absolute horizon. What makes it possible to shift imperceptibly between the two is the idea of *making amends*. To relieve, to improve, is already to *mend* – to some extent – what is wrong. Here, repairing refers to an operation of limited, relative scope – good done within incompleteness (like a handyman doing what he can with whatever tools he has). But when people talk about the Saviour having come 'to make amends for original sin', or when a member of the faithful or a militant Christian embarks upon some form of sacrificial charity, the good is done no longer within incompleteness, it is within completeness (the hoped-for reparation must be a redemption, a revolution).

We shall see in the next and final chapter that the Christ scenario, by its nature lending an aura of unequalled intensity to the idea of the individual, has become intimately blended with the process of emancipation which has marked Western history, and still marks it so deeply. But before broaching this point, I would like to conclude this chapter with reference to a final example, that of a contemporary embodiment of the association between the sense of humanity and the cult of infinitude.

In *Evangelium vitae*, An Encyclical on the Value and Inviolability of Human Life,[18] John Paul II seeks to achieve a broad consensus through an appeal to the moral convictions shared by all people of good will, even non-believers. In this way he points out that everything which is an offence to the dignity of man should be condemned, starting with murder. It is therefore in the name of universal moral values that the Church unceasingly takes up 'the evangelical cry in defence of the world's poor, those who are threatened and despised and whose human rights are violated'. 'Just as a century ago, it was the working classes which were oppressed in the fundamental rights;' nowadays, there exists 'a great multitude of weak and defenceless human beings, unborn children in particular, whose fundamental right to life is being trampled upon'.[19] In the sequence of his argument, John Paul II plays constantly on what strikes many readers as an ambiguity. In keeping with the moral message of the Gospel, the Pope makes an appeal to compassion – an appeal that is meant to touch all men of good will; he then slips imperceptibly from respect for the *person* to respect for *life* (a notion that is highly valued by Christianity: Christ is resurrected, he is 'the way, and the truth, and the life'; the Eucharist is the 'staff of life'). In this case, *life* designates the human embryo, which, according to Christian theology, is endowed with a soul from the moment of conception.[20] For many people of good will, however, the embryo is not yet a person, is not yet a being conscious of itself. John Paul shifts, therefore, from the moral feeling which connects us to our fellows to respect for all life, as if they were one and the same thing. A respect demanded not because the dignity of the human person is attached to this life, but because, coming directly from the hands of God, it is sacred.

My purpose, one might imagine, is not to situate the position taken by John Paul II within the conventional framework of the controversy over abortion. This, it seems to me, is not the real issue;

to grasp that, one need only recall two essential features of the context in which *Evangelium vitae* was published.

Point one: these days it has become difficult, and and perhaps even impossible, to propose the prospect of a personal immortality as the main axis for the expectations and, above all, the duties of the faithful. Even good Christians have become increasingly reluctant to to put their trust in the hereafter at the expense of life in this world (only recently, moreover, some eminent American theologians made a pronouncement against the immortality of the soul). In these circumstances, it becomes problematic to attach human beings to a good infinite – something that is essential for Christianity – and the distance which separates Christianity from mere theism becomes dangerously reduced. In his encyclical, John Paul II takes note of this situation by inviting the faithful to approach God not by saving *their own soul*, but by saving *souls*, innocent, defenceless souls, lives within the province of the other world not because they occur *after* earthly life, but *before* it.

Point two: humanity, as we know, is now facing an unprecedented population problem. In this respect, the invention of contraceptives has come none too soon. The Pope rejects contraception. However, he cannot condemn it too insistently either. First, that would in fact come down to prescribing birth control by means of sexual abstinence – a message which, experience shows, is increasingly hard to get through. Then, the alternative solution of preaching multiplication at full tilt (new souls for the Lord) would appear too irresponsible. Finally, the loss of tiny beings who could have been conceived but were not (because of contraception) has little to commend it to the imagination. The foetus, however – a being which can be photographed! – contains significant possibilities in this respect, so that John Paul II can even invite the faithful to see in the murdered embryo or foetus a tragic echo of Christ's death. Jesus is nailed to the cross, he reminds us: 'he experiences the moment of his greatest "powerlessness", and his life seems completely delivered to the derision of his adversaries and into the hands of his executioners. . . . And yet, precisely amid all this, having seen him breathe his last, the Roman centurion exclaims: "Truly this man was the Son of God!" ' Thus the glory of

Christ is revealed, '*on the cross his glory is made manifest*'. '*From the Cross, the source of life, the "people of life" is born and increases.*'[21] Killing a foetus therefore, in a sense, amounts to recrucifying Christ. Better instead to revere the Son of God in the human embryo, and thus to subordinate our earthly well-being to the absolute value of Life.

The embryo or the foetus commended to our devotion must therefore prevail over the compassion we might feel towards those millions of human lives which reproductive irresponsibility spills out across the planet and which, we know, are doomed to poverty and pain. The essential point here is not that the Pope condemns abortion (we cannot, after all, expect him to approve of it!); the essential point is that by turning the unborn child into a holy cause, the Pope, in his delicate management of the relations between Christianity's humanity and its inhumanity, relegates to the shadows the sufferings endured by the huge mass of human beings whose lives are no less sacred than that of the foetus.

9

The Promethean Revolt:
Emancipatory Ideal and Confrontational Stance

In Chapter 6, on William Godwin's *roman à thèse*, we saw how, with the coming of Enlightenment ideas, on the one hand the novel was called upon to illustrate and exalt the emancipatory ideal of the individual; but, on the other, the aspects whereby narrative touches upon the bad infinite are defused by being placed under the heading of aesthetic values (in particular that of the sublime). As we also saw, it is not difficult to find the reason for this division: if it is true that human beings are at the mercy of limitlessness, then the modern conception of the individual, supported by the euphemistic version of the infinite in the person of God, must be called into question, and with it the emancipatory ideal of the individual.

Among the narratives which illustrate this emancipatory ideal, those whose theme is the Promethean revolt occupy a privileged place. The subtitle of *Frankenstein, The Modern Prometheus*, has not failed to intrigue critical interpreters. Those who are unable to resist the temptation of branding the novel with the plot of the sorcerer's apprentice have concluded that Mary Shelley had intended to warn against the excesses of a Promethean outlook. This interpretation has the drawback of reducing the novel to the scope of a moral fable, thus offering a fresh illustration of the universal desire to undermine the living power of narrative for the sake of a reasonable approach. It is true, however, that Victor Frankenstein is a Prometheus, in the sense that he steals the spark of life from the gods and gives form to a human being (like the

Prometheus *plasticator* who was familiar to the Graeco-Roman world and restored to a place of honour during the Renaissance). But we have seen that the monster who excites the reader's pity is also a Prometheus, a Prometheus subjected to torture, who, like the bound Prometheus, revolts and curses its master. As for the fact that both of them are driven by this challenge to rush to their destruction, it does not mean that Mary Shelley's moral purpose was to condemn Promethean audacity but, rather, that she proved herself capable of seeing its intensity through to the very end. Lastly, the poet Shelley would not have given *Frankenstein* his endorsement (as he did by encouraging Mary to write it, by reading over her text and composing a preface for it himself) had it been the young woman's intention to repudiate Prometheus. In fact, Shelley identified with the Titan,[1] and in 1818, at the time when *Frankenstein* appeared, was writing a long poem on the glory of Prometheus (already celebrated two years earlier by his friend Byron). Moreover, the liberating challenge of Prometheus must have been all the more present in the Shelleys' minds, given that in England at the time ferocious repressive measures were being taken against working-class and democratic protest.

In this chapter, I offer some remarks on the emancipatory ideal as related to the figure of Prometheus and some of his descendants. In the course of the brilliant career he enjoyed throughout the Romantic period, Prometheus displayed features which gave him a kinship as much with the biblical character of Job as with the Platonic allegory of the cave, with Milton's Satan as with Jesus. What is at issue within the modern embodiments of the Titan, in that great figure of the *innocent culprit*, lies in modernity's answers to the question of what it is to be oneself, along with the individual's relation to completeness and, obviously, our conception of emancipation. My goal, in the pages that follow, is to show that the Western ideal of the emancipation of the individual does not rest just upon openly defended values such as liberty and justice, but also upon a scenario of confrontation in which the bad infinite plays a part – but an unspoken one. By offering a critique of the ideal of emancipation, I would like to contribute to a task which is very necessary in our own day, that of rethinking this ideal in order to

stop it from getting stuck in a combination of laziness and arro-
gance (the complacency of preaching to the whole world values
which we instantly present as universal, without asking ourselves
why we are so fond of them).

So, before I stop to consider Shelley's Prometheus and some
other examples which illustrate the stance of the modern hero, I
would like to point out the essential features which, it seems to me,
constitute the bedrock of the ideal of emancipation.

As they spread the movement for emancipation which runs
through their history, Europeans have represented this movement
to themselves in a simple and universal form: the value of the
individual, his right to liberty, and his power to think for himself
become progressively freed from the shackles of tradition and the
yoke of oppression. In singing the praises of this fine epic, European culture tends to forget what it owes to a pre-construction
which happens not be universal. This pre-construction is the difference between two levels of reality. These levels have a variety of
names, but through this diversity the permanence of the difference
between them is apparent: God and the world below, Being and
becoming, transcendence and immanence, the spiritual and the
material, the body and the soul, the authentic self and the artifice
of society, the essential and the contingent, the absolute and the
relative, the infinite and the finite, and so on. This series of
oppositions, as elaborated by philosophy and Christianity, has deep
roots in European tradition, but is nonetheless alien to Chinese
thought and to the majority of non-monotheistic conceptions. The
ideal of emancipation always involves a passage from one level of
reality to the other. Even if at first sight this appears contradictory,
emancipation is just as much a movement from this world on earth
to a higher one as vice versa. Let us take one example. The biblical
narrative of the Israelites' flight from Egypt provided a commonplace analogy of liberation for the Puritans (and later for the slaves
in the United States). One political tract distributed in 1659 by
English revolutionaries proclaims: 'We are upon a march from
Egypt to Canaan, from a land of bondage and darkness to a land of
liberty and rest.'[2] The Promised Land assumes the aspect of a
heavenly land if it is where Yahweh leads his elect. But at the same

time the revolutionaries make reference to the power of the conservative Episcopal Church as an 'Egyptian tyranny'; from this point of
view, the flight from Egypt is a release from the yoke of theocracy,
allowing the attainment of a secular freedom. In an analogous way,
the French Revolution proclaims the overturning of power from on
High, and repudiates the religious justifications for the hierarchical
social order, so as to replace it with a profane power that issues
from below – in other words, from the people. But at the same
time, the hopes which the revolutionaries place in the coming of a
'regenerated' society and of a 'new man' (an expression taken from
Saint Paul) continue to proclaim the Kingdom of God, albeit with
another inflection.

We can observe this same double movement when we shift from
political emancipation to that of the person. Thinking for oneself
means depending upon natural reason instead of subordinating
oneself to Revelation. And the Protestant fostering of the individual
rests, as we know, upon a justification of his fulfilment in this world
(hence the rejection of the monastic life which, in the opinion of a
Protestant, in no way prefigures the heavenly city). But this humanist restoration of profane values is combined with a movement in
the opposite direction, since the emancipation of the individual
rests equally upon the transcendence affirmed by his interiority. In
the view of the Calvinists, the profane gratifications which man
draws from nature are the result of a right conferred upon him
directly by God, whose power as creator is thereby reinforced by
man.[3] Similarly for Kant, whose morality is emblematic of the
modern spirit: if I must treat others as an end and not as a means,
this is not because some fundamental bond of coexistence joins me
to them; it is out of pure respect for the Law which roots my inner
being in Reason and the invisible world.

The Western conception of emancipation therefore corresponds
to a reshaping of the relationship between immanence and transcendence. This reshaping, as we have just seen, is expressed in a
double movement distinguished by an impulse to liberty: on the
one hand, to make available to human action in this world forces
which have been hitherto defined and managed within the framework of the world above; on the other, to underline the indepen-

dent (therefore inner) character of a form of transcendence anchored in the self. What is at issue in this redistribution is the question of the fulfilment of the self; but, as I have stressed throughout this study, any answer to this question involves certain forms of compromise between coexistence and completeness. But, the ideal of emancipation is unable to make any explicit recognition of the constitutive character of the tension between these two poles, since what is involved here is precisely to guarantee the representation of human beings and of society in which this tension disappears.

The essential point about what is inherently unthought in this ideal of emancipation can now be brought to light: if, as I wished to show in the preceding chapters, the real infinite can only be the bad infinite (destructive boundlessness), then the belief in a higher level of reality (transcendence, the good infinite, the authentic self, etc.), far from reaching the site of truth, is the fruit of an adjustment which disguises it. *The good infinite is the euphemism we need in order to achieve compatibility between our absolute sense of ourselves and the bonds of coexistence.* I am not claiming that it is possible to give up all idealizations of the infinite; that would amount to claiming that I myself have gone beyond this propensity, and that I can denounce an illusion of which the rest of mankind remains a prisoner – a ridiculous pretension, since it would be dependent upon the very desire from which it would pronounce itself freed. What I do claim, on the contrary, is that, in order to begin rethinking our ideas about emancipation (or, more generally, the forms of fulfilment which are accessible and desirable for human beings), it is necessary:

1. to take into account the bad infinite in the representation we make of ourselves – in other words, to stop acting as if our relation to completeness stopped short at a connection to a good infinite, or even to a form of Reason devoid of all infinitude;
2. to call into question the very distinction between two levels of reality – a distinction which, as it has been constructed and perpetuated within Western thought, promotes the idea that the

level of the ideal, or of 'authenticity', *transcends* that of existing material and social reality.

We can now understand how the split between two levels of reality leads to thinking of emancipation in the dualist form of a confrontation in which the axis of completeness always merges with the Good. We can likewise understand why *ideas* about emancipation are twinned with a *narrative* – a narrative which is presented like a simple transfer of these ideas (a picture of a reality as conceived by these ideas, or a fiction illustrating, defending or symbolizing these ideas); but a narrative which in reality, deploying the grandeur of an unconditional affirmation of the self, gives rise to an exalted and, to some extent, obscure adherence to this stance.

The hero of this type of narrative, whether it be Prometheus or some other character, comes into contact with the sublime in his solitary confrontation with omnipotence. He then is shown, according to the variants of the standard scenario, as:

• *unjustly crushed* (like Jesus, or Job, or the blind and shackled Samson, or Prometheus, also bound and tortured);
• *unrecognized* (like the character imagined by Plato, who, after leaving the cave, and having moved from the shadows to their intrinsic reality, rejoins his fettered companions; or like Jesus, doomed to the infamy of the cross like a common criminal, but in his invisible interiority the Son of God);
• *a rebel* (like the Satan of *Paradise Lost* and some of the Romantics or, yet again, like Prometheus);
• and *a liberator* (this being a leader, a Titan, or a revolutionary).

Let us take a closer look at one of the narratives of this type, Shelley's *Prometheus Unbound*, and let us compare it to Aeschylus' *Prometheus Bound*. Like other Romantics who came after them, Mary and Percy Shelley expressed great admiration for Aeschylus' tragedy. Reading *Prometheus Bound* in their wake, we can easily guess which passages aroused their enthusiasm. Aeschylus' Prometheus rose up against the rigid harshness of Zeus, and – we discover this in the first lines of the drama – gave fire to men out of philanthropy (Aeschylus is the first Greek author who gives the Titan this significance and turns him into the founder of all civilization).

Simultaneously crushed and triumphant, Prometheus is the very epitome of the sublime figure. No doubt Shelley liked the passage in which Prometheus identifies with Typhon struck down by Zeus's thunderbolt and lying at the foot of Mount Etna: 'high upon whose tops/Hephaestus sits and strikes the flashing ore.'[4] – Typhon vanquished, yet still emitting torrents of lava! The ending of the tragedy must also have aroused his enthusiasm, particularly this passage where we see Prometheus issue a final challenge to Zeus:

> Let the locks of the lightning, all bristling and whitening,
>   Flash, coiling me round,
> While the aether goes surging 'neath thunder and scourging
>   of wild winds unbound!
> Let the blast of the firmament whirl from its place
>   The earth rooted below,
> And the brine of the ocean, in rapid emotion,
>   Be driven in the face
> Of the stars up in heaven, as they walk to and fro!
> Let him hurl me anon into Tartarus – on –
>   To the blackest degree,
> With Necessity's vortices strangling me down;
> But he cannot join death to a fate meant for *me*![5]

At this point the Oceanides refuse to abandon the daring Prometheus to his suffering, and the tragedy concludes in a cosmic upheaval in which the forces of chaos erupt: the earth quakes, an abyss yawns, and the bound Prometheus is swallowed up amid thunderclaps and furious winds.

A passage of this kind lends itself to the Romantics' reading of the drama. For it is precisely when he is reduced to nothing that the Romantic hero – who is always to some extent Christlike – achieves his fulfilment; it is when he comes face to face with destruction that he finally coincides with his own infinitude. Thus, as we have seen, Frankenstein's creature immolating itself amid the wild and icy wastes of the pole. Or else, later on, Captain Ahab nailed to his Leviathan, the huge white whale which drags him into the depths of the ocean. Or, earlier, Rousseau – Rousseau persecuted and dispossessed as Caleb Williams will be, and, like him, crying out: 'The whole of human might is now powerless against me. . . .' Jean Starobinski, who quotes this phrase (which was written by Rousseau on a playing card), adds aptly: 'The infinite power discovered by Jean-Jacques is the power of being himself in an unconditional way, once all adverse conditions have accumulated.'[6]

Shelley's Prometheus, too, will defy Jupiter by turning his torture into a declared triumph:

> . . . torture and solitude,
> Scorn and despair, – these are mine empire: –
> More glorious far than that which thou surveyest.

Thus, one might believe that what separates Shelley from Aeschylus is merely the Christlike features and the breath of revolution with which the English poet creates an aura for Prometheus. When a secondary character points out to Prometheus the torments suffered by Christ, the Titan in Shelley's poem declares that he wants to be 'The saviour and the strength of suffering man'. As for Shelley's admiration for the French Revolution, this emerges clearly when, for example, Prometheus predicts the overturning and downfall of the tyrant Jupiter:

> . . . Thine Infinity shall be
> A robe of envenomed agony;
> And thine Omnipotence a crown of pain.

Jupiter, for his part, expresses his fear of humanity:

> The soul of man, like unextinguished fire,
> Yet burns towards heaven with fierce reproach . . .
> Hurling up insurrection, which might make
> Our antique empire insecure.

No doubt it was Shelley's inention to extend and enrich the figure
of the philanthropist in revolt as portrayed by Aeschylus in the first
half of the fifth century BC. But in reality – and I want to stress this
point – the problematic within which Aeschylus' tragedy was
inscribed is radically different from the modern ideology to which
Shelley subscribes: Aeschylus ascribes no less importance to justice
than we do, but he does not conceive of it as we do. Or rather: what
is different in Aeschylus is his conception of the human being.
When a conflict develops around an injustice, each of the two
parties tends to adopt a confrontational stance. Aeschylus pays a
great deal of attention to what is involved in this stance of self-
affirmation in direct relation to the other. When we are caught up
in a conflict, we run a strong risk of misrecognizing the tension or
the division inherent in our desire – the desire for coexistence and
for justice, but at the same time a desire to overwhelm and crush
the other. In our awareness of ourselves, this division tends to
become blurred since the frontier between the two desires is not
inside us; instead it appears to us to be *outside* us; as far as we can
see, it merges with the frontier which separates us from the other
party. Thus, once embarked upon a scenario of confrontation, each
of the two parties involved has a perception of being endowed with
a wholeness (and consequently with a self-gratification) which the
state of peace does not confer. What is important to Aeschylus is
that if, at the start of the conflict, one of the parties is fully in the
right, the relationship of confrontation will drive this party to *exceed*
what is just. The idea of justice is opposed to the idea of injustice;
Prometheus is opposed to Zeus. For Aeschylus, what is tragic about
this is precisely that the pairing of the concepts and the pairing of
the characters do not coincide, and cannot be superimposed.
Between the idea of justice and the characters who claim to act in
its name a discrepancy arises – a discrepancy to which each of the
two protagonists *remains blind*, but which is *visible from the viewpoint
of a third party*.[7] In Shelley's poem, however, Prometheus embodies
not just one of the two parties, but also the third: his vision of the
conflict becomes merged with the superior point of view of justice
and truth. This is why, for him, the coming of justice has no need
of any mediating character; it is in the context of a duel to the

death that justice will triumph. (The same would go for Sartre's adaptation of Euripides' *The Trojans*; as Nicole Loraux stresses, Sartre was to give this tragedy a Manichaean character which it did not have in the Greek text, thus aligning it with the preface he had written for Fanon's *The Wretched of the Earth*.[8])

In Aeschylus, the third-party position has its embodiment in the chorus, in Hephaestus (to whom Zeus has given the task of binding Prometheus, but who is reluctant to carry out the sentence), in Oceanus or in Hermes. The chorus speaks of 'Zeus, the stern and cold,/Whose law is taken from his breast'.[9] This is the violent Zeus of the world's beginnings; he is at the mercy of overweening pride [*hubris*], and has not yet learned to bend to justice [*dike*]. Speaking of their new master's excessive harshness, which Hephaestus and Hermes deplore as much as he does, Prometheus notes with sagacity that 'maturing Time/teaches all things'.[10] But these third parties who show the bound Titan their sympathy nonetheless do not take his side; Prometheus also goes too far. 'I loathe the universal gods,' Prometheus declares to Hermes. 'Thou art raving,' the latter replies. And he adds: 'If thou wert prosperous/Thou wouldst be unendurable.' The chorus, addressing the tortured rebel, endorses the messenger of the gods: 'Our Hermes suits his reasons to the times;/At least I think so, since he bids thee drop/Self-will for prudent counsel. Yield to him!'[11] Likewise, Oceanus, while he is touched by the unjust fate that has fallen to Prometheus, nevertheless deplores his defiant attitude. 'I would fain/Exhort thee . . . to a better wisdom/Titan, know thyself,/And take new softness to thy manners.'[12] Know thyself – in other words, learn to see yourself from the point of view of the third party, and thereby recognize that the frontier which separates the just from the unjust is not just between you and Zeus, but also *within you*, with the result that your desire leads you to both justice and excess.

In Aeschylus' *Prometheus Bound*, the third-party mediators do not succeed in bringing the conflict out of the relationship of confrontation in which it is enmeshed. As the tragedy reaches its conclusion, Zeus and Prometheus, intoxicated by their posture of omnipotence, persist in the unconditional assertion of themselves, in the duel for all or nothing. In *Prometheus Unbound*, a tragedy which is lost, Aeschylus intended to show the triumph of justice through a reconciliation reached by the gods and the Titan. A conclusion which, one suspects, would have been repugnant to Shelley; for him, it was a matter not of succeeding in stepping outside the relation of the duel, but of winning within it.

How did the transition from the Prometheus of Antiquity to the modern Prometheus come about? In order to answer this question briefly, there are two essential points to consider.[13]

First, the ambiguous position of the Titan, halfway between gods and men. By stealing fire from the gods in order to give it to men, Prometheus, although he is immortal, appears to align himself on the side of men. Yet, from the fourth century BC onwards, the figure of Prometheus also stands as a creator of humanity: he makes men out of earth and water (fire, then, is no longer merely culinary and technical; it gives creatures life). It is by recourse to this ambiguous status that the Romantic Prometheus will blend together the Titan and the human, the creator and the creature, hubris and justice.

Secondly, the comparison in operation between the myth of Prometheus and the Genesis story. On the basis of successive medieval compilations, a number of Renaissance treatises read Greek mythology as disguised biblical truths. Thus, for Henri Estienne, the first man made by Prometheus was Adam, and Pandora was Eve. The fire stolen from the gods corresponds to the forbidden fruit which gives a knowledge of good and evil, and the revolt of Prometheus corresponds to that of man, who, by committing original sin, rebels against divine order. Other authors like Boccaccio, Filippo Villani or Marsilio Ficino see in Prometheus, instead, the civilizing hero who brings the arts to fallen humanity. Pico della Mirandola, for his part, underlines the Promethean power that God gave to man, the power to shape himself. Galileo would speak, in his *Dialogo sopra i due massimi sistemi*, of the artist as a second creator, 'a true Prometheus under Jupiter'. In 1710, in *Soliloquy, or Advice to an Author*, Shaftesbury would renew the formula; if the painter and the sculptor imitate, the true poet creates: 'Such a Poet is indeed a second Maker, a just Prometheus under Jove.'

We can therefore understand how, having rejected the dogma of original sin, Enlightenment philosophy should justify Prometheus' rebellion against Zeus. Voltaire was the first (in *Pandore* [1740]) to turn Jupiter into a tyrant who persecuted humanity. Prometheus shakes off this yoke and fights the god on his own ground. 'Dare to shape a soul,' writes Voltaire, addressing the Titan, 'and be a creator in your own right.' Thirty years later, it was Goethe's turn to exalt Prometheus. From that point on, Prometheus is no longer a figure split between one character who is close to the gods and another who is close to men; he incarnates the divine element in man. For *Sturm und Drang* he was the supreme hero, at one and the same time a political rebel and a creative artist (no longer *under* Jupiter, but *the equal* of God). Marx was to write, in 1841, that in the yearbook of philosophy Prometheus occupied the highest rank among the saints and martyrs.[14] Schlegel, Byron, Hugo and, of course, Shelley all praised Aeschylus to the skies – but, as we have seen, they ignored the essence of his problematic, and encapsulated the third-party position, which alone can distinguish the just from the unjust, within that of Prometheus, who thereby becomes fully justified.

With Shelley, the reader is therefore no longer invited to take the position of a third party who would be torn between compassion for the fate inflicted on the Titan and the alienating effect of his blindness and hubris. The reader is no longer invited to take to heart Oceanus' injunction to Prometheus in Aeschylus' tragedy: Know thyself. The reader (as we saw seen in Chapter 5, on the pity inspired by Frankenstein's creature) is now invited to become inscribed within the 'triangle of moral relations' – a triangle which is very different from the one that had been formed by Zeus, Prometheus and the third party, since compassion henceforth authorizes the last of these to identify without reservation with a figure who, in the Christlike position of total victim, is totally affirmed. (Nowadays, in a similar manner, television programmes with a humanitarian outlook give credence to the idea that whenever a conflict arises, the most important thing is to determine who are the victims, and thus to provide the viewers with a good object of compassion.)

All this comes about, therefore, as if, until now, the progress of emancipation had been able to take place only at the cost of a certain intellectual regression. With Enlightenment philosophy, we witness – as Paul Bénichou has demonstrated so well[15] – the birth of a secular spiritual power. Among the representatives of this power – which was in part snatched from the clergy, and forms an artistic and literary intellectual elite – the stance of the rebel (or that of the pariah, as it will be called in the nineteenth century) tends to merge with the place of whoever intervenes in the name of transcendent values. For Christ and for those who speak in his name, the final truths are affirmed in a rupture with those of this world. In their wake, the representatives of secular spiritual power will criticize society from the depths of their inner being, a place which is supposed to be external and superior to this society because it is founded on the universal principles of morality and nurtured by the objectivity of knowledge.[16] As defenders of the ideal of emancipation, they dramatize this ideal (and they dramatize themselves) through narratives and scenarios of confrontation.

The effect produced by these *narratives* on their readers is supposed to have no other source but the *ideas* in the service of which they are placed (just as, in the past, the rhetorical force of an edifying discourse was supposed to emanate from the very truths of religion). As a result, the particular effect of these narratives (the supplement of pleasure which they furnish independently of the ideas) is smuggled through. Thus, what characterizes the Western ideal of emancipation and makes it so seductive is that, because of what is unintentional in these scenarios, the human propensity to derive gratification from confrontation assumes a kind of camou-flage and finds a legitimation which are, so to speak, unexpected. Certainly, the process of civilization, of more lenient practices and of more peaceful relations, whose significance in the history of modern Europe has been stressed by Norbert Elias, drew support from emancipatory ideas;[17] because he was more closely policed, the individual was also more independent; because it was more democratic, society gave less violent forms to social injustice. How-ever, the ideal of emancipation also provided a means of compen-sation, an outlet for this process of civilization, by preserving in refined forms postures and scenarios of confrontation which in themselves were rather crude.

In order to give some idea of the continuity which was thereby maintained between, on the one hand, unpretentious narratives intended for mass consumption and, on the other, those conceived with a sophisticated elite in mind, undoubtedly the simplest thing is to begin with an example.

As a child, I saw Cecil B. de Mille's *Samson and Delilah.* Victor Mature played the part of Samson (I had already made the acquaintance of this actor in one or two other films – biblical epics – and I was very taken with his style as the muscle-man standing on his dignity). I can remember the final scene of *Samson and Delilah.* Samson blind and in chains, Samson humiliated, Samson turned into an object of derision for the Philistines (like the savage King Kong transformed into a fairground attraction). And then Samson in Dagon's temple, asking a young boy to lead him between the two great pillars and managing to bring them down; Samson as the instrument of God's wrath, and the heavy stones of the temple descending upon the crowd of Philistines. What satisfaction, what jubilation! After seeing the film, I relived this scene of omnipotence by describing it to my brothers and sisters and by acting it out, and, among the horde of terror-stricken Philistines, I imagined some of the adults who held authority over me.

Samson and Delilah has a place among numerous action films which littered my youth. In all these films – Westerns, tales of chivalry, Viking or spy stories – one man has to face another or several others and, usually, kills them. When I became an adult, one thing I noticed about these Westerns was that in some of them the hero sets out to impose the civilizing benefits of the written law and the courtroom upon backwoods settlers who know only gun-fights and revenge killings. Nevertheless, this apparently atypical hero never truly takes it upon himself to play the role of mediator, and never occupies the place of that third party to which Greek tragedy accorded such importance. He always ends up wreathed in glory after drawing his pistol like the rest, and mowing down the villains.[18] The American hero is not a mediator who re-establishes justice by pacifying a conflict and striving to prevent evil from coming about. The evil is done, and he punishes it (for instance, there is 'a cop with somewhat unorthodox methods' – in other words, rough stuff). Beaten, humiliated and persecuted at the beginning, he finally stands up for himself, clears his name and takes his revenge. Have not Samson and other heroes or prophets in the Bible given him an example? (Maybe there are American films in which the issue of justice and injustice is not conveyed through a scenario of confrontation, but I have yet to see any.)

I have just underlined the continuity between the story of Samson and countless films intended for popular consumption. But the link between this biblical character and the ideal of emancipation is no less powerful. Milton – one of the great promoters of this ideal, who was in the vanguard of the political struggles of his day, and whose goal was 'the liberation of all human life from slavery' – wrote a *Samson Agonistes*. The culmination of the poem is also the destruction of Dagon's temple by the blind but redeemed hero (Milton himself was blind). The Philistines are idolaters. They therefore resemble the poet's own adversaries, who are also idolaters, since they regard royalty as sacred and bow to the Pope.[19] In *Paradise Lost*, Satan stands up against God with the aim of overthrowing him. Samson assaults the abode of a god, if not God himself. And he succeeds where Satan fails. For what in Satan was utter darkness has become in Samson the effect of divine power. Samson combats oppression; he is a kind of Prometheus in revolt. Samson sacrifices himself; he is a kind of Christ.

I could equally well show how, for countless writers and intellectuals in the nineteenth and twentieth centuries, the progressive and emancipatory ideal continued to make its appeal to the old scenario of confrontation. I shall limit myself to a few examples. The first ones concern the political aspect of the ideal of emancipation; those that follow concern the aspect of personal fulfilment.

On the political side, there are abundant examples in the history of progressive-revolutionary thought, from the English Civil War right up to our own day. For a general view of the political discourse of confrontation, I refer the reader to Michel Foucault, who has painted an extraordinary picture of it.[20] Foucault contrasts this type of historico-political representation, which he calls 'the discourse of race war', with the juridico-philosophical discourse which draws upon natural Law and the idea of a social contract in order to establish a theory of legitimate sovereignty. With 'the discourse of race war', a discourse of combat, 'we see the outline emerge', says Foucault, 'of something which is fundamentally much closer to the mythico-religious history of the Jews than to the politico-legendary history of the Romans'. And he points out in this context that 'from at least the second half of the Middle Ages onwards, the Bible was the major form within which religious, moral and political objections to the power of kings and the despotism of the Church were articulated'. It is on behalf of this protest-history, this insurrection-history, he adds, 'that revolutionary discourse took its place – that of seventeenth-century England, and that of the nineteenth century in France and the rest of Europe.'[21]

Among the emblematic narratives of emancipation, there is one which has become an obligatory reference for anyone with the slightest claim to know anything about philosophy: 'the master and slave dialectic'. For Alexandre Kojève, in his commentary on Hegel's *Phenomenology of Spirit*, the scenario is explicitly put forward under the heading of an anthropogenesis (a history of the attainment to self-being): 'the relation between Master and Slave,' says Kojève, 'which is to say the first outcome of the "first" human, social and historical contact'.[22] In reality, the scenario corresponds to a situation which is quite specific, that of *a duel without witnesses* (a confrontation without the presence of a third party) – in other words, a variation on the story of Robinson Crusoe and Man Friday. As in *Robinson Crusoe* (which represents the standpoint of the master), or as in *Caleb Williams* (the standpoint of the slave), this is a confrontation between men; in these narratives, there is no room for sexual difference, because it opens up a breach in omnipotence. The absorbing nature of the story told to us by Hegel and Kojève is due precisely to the fact that there is no room for two – at stake, therefore, is omnipotence, insistent but unavowed throughout the whole of their narrative. Because of the narrative tension, and the pathos engendered by this stake of all or nothing, the reader is led to believe that what Hegel and Kojève are describing is indeed the truth – *for an intense feeling is always apt to fuel a conviction of truth.*

Through his confrontation with the master, the slave encounters 'the fear of death, of the absolute Master'.[23] Thus, for the slave, death occupies the place of what, for Job, is omnipotence. And it is because he experiences this confrontation, says Kojève, that the slave is a revolutionary: 'The man who has never experienced the fear of death . . . will act as a "skilful" reformist, not to say a conformist, but never as a real revolutionary.' Indeed, the

> revolutionary transformation of the World presupposes the 'negation', the non-acceptance of the given World as a whole. And at the origin of this absolute negation can only be the absolute terror inspired by the given World, or more precisely by whatever – or whoever – rules over this World, by the Master of this World. So the Master who (involuntarily) engenders the desire for revolutionary negation is the Master of the Slave.[24]

Some of the more recent forms of revolutionary discourse made their appearance in the area of anti-colonial struggle. The ideas of the colonizers, their rhetoric, and the grand narrative figures mobilized by them, are turned against them (the first speech placed in the mouth of an African Moses was written by Prévost in 1735; and in the 1774 edition of the *Histoire des deux Indes*, Diderot hails the coming of a black Spartacus[25]). Thus, in Aimé Césaire, for example, we see a rebellious Black who is not unreminiscent of the monster-rebuked (a character of whom Byron's Cain or Franken-stein's creature offer better examples than Caliban in Shakespeare's *The Tempest*):

> *The Rebel* – My surname: insulted; my first name: humiliated; my state: rebellious; my age: stone age.

> *The Mother* – My race: the human race. My religion: fraternity. . . .

> *The Rebel* – My race: the fallen race. My religion . . . but it will not be you who will be the one to prepare it with your disarmament . . . it is me with my revolt and my poor clenched fists and my wild-haired looks.'[26]

In *Black Skin, White Mask*, Frantz Fanon describes his experience of being designated black in a world of whites:[27] 'Look, Mummy, a Negro, I'm frightened!' Fanon expresses the feeling he then experiences as a brutal dehumanization of his body and appearance, and as a result, the style of the pages which follow is marked with a vengeful exaltation. Reading this passage, I thought of the fury which takes hold of Frankenstein's creature when it perceives that its mere outward appearance provokes the rejection of others. This comparison can give rise to two quite distinct inferences. The first: that the Western conception of the individual – or, rather, his or her dramatization and power of seduction – is expressed in a recurrent manner by the scenario of a violent non-recognition, a situation from which the rejected one draws an acute sense of himself and the additional energy which fuels his stance of insurrection. The second: that Mary Shelley, in writing this kind of scene, was able to express the essence of experiences of non-recognition to which so many human beings are exposed, in reality rather than in fiction.

In *The Wretched of the Earth*, Fanon shows the revolutionary victim of colonization discarding Western ideas. He has been impregnated with them; he has been 'a vigilant sentinel ready to defend the Graeco-Latin pedestal';[28] but 'during the struggle for liberation, at the moment that the native intellectual comes into touch again with his people, this artificial sentinel is turned into dust ... All those speeches seem like collections of dead words.'[29] This does not prevent Fanon from imagining the colonized victim's emancipation in terms of the imposed forms of Western discourse. 'Decolonization is the veritable creation of new men': Saint Paul. 'The last shall be first and the first last':[30] the Gospels. Rid of the colonial bourgeoisie's forms of thought, the militant discovers the people: 'he is literally disarmed by their good faith and honesty';[31] pride and egoism are destroyed; in village assemblies, he sees the simple and spontaneous flowering of the spirit of community and solidarity: this picture of contrasts between good and bad society is already to be seen in Rousseau (in *La Nouvelle Héloïse*), in the edifying pastorals of the late eighteenth century or in the picture of future society which Shelley outlines at the end of his *Prometheus Unbound.*

In the preface he wrote for *The Wretched of the Earth*, Sartre also adopts Fanon's stance of exaltation. The colonized confront the colonizers like the bound Prometheus standing up against the tyranny of Jupiter. With colonial power overturned, 'the minority breed disappears, to be replaced by socialism'.[32] The Sartrean conception of the critical role of the intellectual clearly does not invite the latter to intervene as a third party, but much rather to take sides, as Walzer[33] has stressed. If we consider the exemplary case of resistance against the Nazis, the Sartrean conception of commitment appears to be completely justified, for in this historical situation, even those who in no sense idealized the stance of confrontation could understand that it was their duty to fight against the enemy. However, the Sartrean conception of commitment did not derive only from the example offered by the Resistance, nor only from the revolutionary tradition. It was just as much linked to a particular notion of self-fulfilment.

Like a great many other modern authors, Sartre does not make any very clear distinction between the freedom from oppression and prejudice which consists in 'breaking chains', and the kind which is demonstrated through an unconditional self-affirmation, not to say a claim to some kind of self-genesis; there is nothing surprising about this confusion, since it is at the heart of modern ideology. When I was a teenager I heard, or read, this quotation from Sartre (I still don't know which of his books it comes from): 'Freedom is that part of nothingness which constrains us to make ourselves instead of being.' This proud affirmation struck me as having a very fine ring to it, and when I was eighteen, which was also around the time when I was getting intoxicated on reading *Thus Spake Zarathustra*, I would repeat this phrase of Sartre's to anyone who would listen. (It must be admitted that the formula was designed to please somebody who had just emerged from childhood and an admiration for the figure of Samson, and who was easily seduced by what one might call a phallic use of the word.)

In one of Sartre's plays, *The Flies*, we see Orestes address Jupiter in a way which recalls the challenges launched by Prometheus: 'Foreign to myself – I know it. Outside nature, against nature, without excuse, beyond remedy except what remedy I find within myself. But I shall not return under your Law; I am doomed to have no other law but mine.'[34] In *Sens et non-sens de la révolte,* Julia Kristeva quotes this passage[35] – favourably, it seems. In her book as a whole, noting the power of the contemporary world to absorb us into its invasive compromises, she extols what she calls a 'revolt-culture', a salutary reaction against the levelling of the individual by the tide of media and technology. This idea made me recall Herbert Marcuse's book *One-Dimensional Man* (1968), in which he said that one-dimensional society kept down poetic and metaphysical truths like animals in reserves, so as to avoid their subversive action.[36] Likewise I can remember numerous sermons heard in my childhood, in which the representative of spiritual power warned his flock against their inclination to let themselves be preoccupied by the concerns and compromises of a 'one-dimensional' daily life, exhorting them to awaken and take up the struggle again – in short, to bring themselves face to face with their true being.

This sequence of associations thrown up by a phrase of Sartre's shows where complacency can lead in a constant reiteration of the ideal of emancipation: to conformity and subjugation – subjugation to the old heroic current of Western sermonizing, conformity with regard to old values uncritically recycled.

Simone de Beauvoir employs the rhetoric of heroic authenticity according to the example of a celebrated reprobate, the Marquis de Sade. Sade entered the writers' pantheon in the 1950s. Not, of course, without difficulty – it took some advanced thinkers to come to his defence. This meant a resumption of service for the confrontational stance of which Shelley and, even more so, Byron were the emblematic heroes. A combination of morality within political struggle and immoralism in the affirmation of the self: a dual mode of fighting against an unjust and prejudiced society. Sade, says de Beauvoir, 'went beyond the sensualism of his day and turned it into a morality of authenticity'. In her long article on the Marquis, de Beauvoir seems to take his philosophical expositions at face value. At any rate, she turns him into someone who has deliberately and voluntarily settled on his path: 'Against indifference *he chose* cruelty.'[37] Here we should open a parenthesis to recall something that Greek tragedy was aware of, and that our voluntarism tends to forget: in whichever direction we find ourselves driven to develop the affirmation of ourselves, the very force which drives us invites us to tell ourselves that we are not constrained by it but that, on the contrary, we are the ones acting voluntarily; in fact it would be painful for us to admit that *we do not have the power to govern the way in which our power affirms itself.* Voluntarism – the fantasy of mastery – when it is expressed within the proud declarations which Shelley places in the mouth of Prometheus, strikes us nowadays as somewhat puerile. And probably the Byronic posture also seemed somewhat out of date to the authors who exalted Sadeian subversion in the 1950s. But that did not stop some of them from making the most of the opportunity offered by de Sade to take up this posture anew. For it is not the posture which becomes outmoded, merely the discourses within which it is enacted. When, with the passing of time, these discourses lose their subversive novelty, thereby exposing the naivety hidden by their outer covering of hardness, people take their distance, imagining that they have lost their liking for the stance that lies behind them. Not in the slightest; this is reborn and perpetuated under fresh guises.

In the stance of self-assertion, the illusion of voluntarism is matched by a misrecognition of transgression. Jean Paulhan's statements about de Sade amply demonstrate this. In 1956, the publication of de Sade's works by Éditions Pauvert gave rise to a case involving outrage to public decency. When this happened, Paulhan made a statement in which he explained to Maître Maurice Garçon that 'Sade lived at a time when a somewhat woolly philosophy accepted unreservedly that man was good and that he only had to be restored to his original nature for everything to turn out well. This led Sade to maintain, on the contrary, that man was wicked, and to demonstrate in detail, in every manner, this wickedness which he posited initially on sexuality.'

The following exchange ensued:

The presiding judge – I should like you to explain to us wherein you see the purity of this philosophy, which strikes me as destructive.

J. Paulhan – There is a purity in destruction. As Saint-Just said. . . .

The presiding judge – Don't you think that the purity of destruction is a danger to public morals?

J. Paulhan – It is dangerous. I knew a young woman who entered a convent after she had read Sade's works, and because she had read them.[38]

Here we can see the reflective level of ideas contaminated and, so to speak, absorbed into the non-conscious level of the stance (which is a scenario set in motion by the affirmation of self). In his defence of de Sade, Paulhan relies at first on a philosophical thesis – the same as the one which I maintain in this book: de Sade had good grounds for rejecting the widespread wrong-headedness of Enlightenment thought. But since at the same time, in Paulhan's view, de Sade represents revolt against the established order, a stance which he makes his own, then to defend de Sade is to follow his example. De Sade, dangerous? Yes, but only for those who retreat before a 'the purity of destruction' – that is to say, those who take refuge in bigotry. With his story of the young woman in the convent, Paulhan stands before the presiding judge like de Sade himself challenging the established order. Paulhan has imperceptibly shifted from a reflection on wickedness to a confrontational stance.

By thereby eliding the level of ideas with that of the scenario, Paulhan elides the *observation* (in human beings there is a propensity to evil) with the *value judgement* (it is good to exercise this evil, even if – or because – it is repugnant to bourgeois pusillanimity).

There is an inherent confusion both in the ambiguity of the qualifier 'good' and in the nature of the evil concerned. As Lacan has stressed, de Sade shows that we can find 'happiness in evil', not only in good – an insight which Freud was able to turn to his advantage.[39] However, de Sade's work does not, strictly speaking, constitute the 'inaugural' point of a subversion; the idea of self-fulfilment in evil was already familiar to the Augustinian conception of human beings, and it is expressed in the most radical and most flagrant way in the cry of Milton's Satan: 'Evil, be thou my good!'.[40]

It is obvious that within the Augustinian perspective, the fulfilment experienced in doing evil is not morally good. For Paulhan and others, the distinction between the two meanings of the word 'good' is blurred; at the same time, the evil in question, which supposedly brings self-fulfilment, shifts from the register of an actually destructive cruelty (for instance, the evils which, according to Las Casas, the Spanish inflicted on the Indians[41]) to a form of cruelty which is exercised in the field of sexual freedom. This shift takes place in silence – in part through the idea, a would-be Freudian one, that human wickedness must be founded on sexuality (consequently, this wickedness is not as wicked as all that). In part, too, through an opposition to Christian puritanism (puritanism erred in condemning sexuality, and the time has come to assert it as a good and a freedom).

Ultimately, the idea of transgression as a *real* movement towards destruction does not hold up. Precisely because literature has the power to bring to life the reality of boundlessness within a text, the writer would like to believe that he is transgressing in earnest, whereas he is in fact engaging in aesthetic or erotic transgressions. As a result, the difference between the appearance and the reality of boundlessness is erased. This is an erasure which arrives, by a different route, at the one which is the outcome of wrong-headedness itself. The puritanism of good feeling makes man innocent: at heart his desire is supposedly for good. Since it is aesthetic, Paulhan's view of transgression, like Bataille's (and, earlier Shelley's and Byron's), also makes man innocent: no true transgression can exist, since the barrier crossed is, in the end, merely the social barrier of prejudices and mediocrity. By assuming guilt, one therefore remains innocent – and even attains a superior kind of purity.

The figure of the innocent guilty party confers the greatest grandeur upon the confrontational stance linked to the ideal of emancipation. The work introduced by Michel Foucault, *I, Pierre Riviere, having slaughtered my mother, my sister and my brother . . .,*[42] is an outstanding illustration of this figure. In Normandy, in 1835, a twenty-year-old peasant killed his mother, his sister and his younger brother. In prison he composed a text which was not his confession but what he had planned to write *before* committing his triple crime. This, therefore, comes to light as the fruit of a long and silent fermentation. It had been the young man's intention to conclude his action by taking his own life. In prison he saw himself as already dead; he hanged himself in 1840.

His family's hardships are described in his memoir. The arduous life led by his grandmother, whose husband had been sick and infirm for the last twenty-five years, only one of her four children then surviving, this being the father of Pierre Rivière, a man who was the object of his own wife's hatred, humiliated and persecuted by her ('the constant sufferings he endured', writes Pierre Rivière). And once more the lament delivered up by the Mesopotamian tablets and addressed by Job to Yahweh: 'Oh, she said, weeping . . . I wish I was dead and buried, have I had to go through so much misery in my life to be rewarded like this; why does the good Lord bring down so much suffering.'[43] And the young man upon whom falls the weight of these sufferings, a young man intolerably torn between being nothing and being everything:

– 'My behaviour was sometimes odd. My schoolfellows noticed this and laughed at me; I ascribed their contempt to some foolish actions I thought I had committed at the start, and which dogged me and discredited me once and for all.'
– 'I was consumed by notions of my own greatness and immortality; I judged myself far above others.'

The fantasy of the reversal of nothing into everything therefore grips Pierre Rivière – a reversal which was to be enacted through revenge and suicide ('to take my revenge on all of those people'). 'I devised the dreadful project that I carried out. . . . It even seemed to me that God had destined me for this and that I wreaked justice for him.' In order to challenge iniquitous human laws, models have to be drawn from great examples of sacrifice. Just like one of the Maccabees, who killed an elephant on which rode the enemy king, 'although he knew he would be suffocated beneath this animal's weight' (like Samson beneath the stone pillars of the Philistines' temple). And Our Lord Jesus Christ, who 'died on the cross to save all mankind and redeem them from enslavement to the devil, sin and eternal damnation'. As he himself says, Pierre Rivière harbours ideas of the *sublime*.

In order to force fate – the impossibility of existence – and, ultimately, to make good, to affirm himself in a blinding flash, Pierre Rivière embarks upon the old scenario of sublimity within destructive confrontation. 'A *martyr*, in his own view of himself; a *monster*, in the considered opinion of his judges,' one Calvados newspaper was to write.

What are the figures summoned around Pierre Rivière by Foucault and his collaborators? They are more modern figures, not inspired by the Bible, but nonetheless deriving from the same scenario as the one within which the young man had inscribed himself.

Like Frankenstein's creature, 'the other (an indigenous savage or a country bumpkin) cannot be named . . ., as a man he is absolutely nothing. All that is left to him then is the possibility of inverting values . . . In order for him to be heard, he must kill.' The peasants are oppressed and crushed exactly as are those described by Michelet in *La sorcière*. Like the witch, some of them rebel. They take a stand and sacrifice themselves. 'Here murder is an exemplary event whose target in a rigid world is the timelessness of oppression and the order of power.'[44] In his introduction to the work, Foucault writes: 'out of some kind of veneration, and perhaps also from terror of a text which was to carry off four deaths with it, we did not wish to superimpose our own text on the memory of Pierre Rivière. We were subjugated by the red-eyed parricide.' In the text by Simone de Beauvoir to which I have referred, she quotes from de Sade: 'Crime has a grandeur and *sublimity* of nature which wins out and always will win out over the monotonous attractions of virtue.'[45] In the same issue of *Les Temps modernes* in which de Beauvoir's article appeared, René Étiemble had an article on the Rimbaud myth: 'the adventurer, the madman, the criminal and the poet assassinated', he writes. And he shows how, after Rimbaud, other great figures will embody each one of these qualifications with the same halo of idealization. The criminal is Genet: the 'sacred nature of the criminal, to which, throughout his entire work, Genet strives to give substance'.[46]

For Foucault, Pierre Rivière is a kind of Genet; and Genet himself, in his own eyes, is a kind of Christ. In her study of him,

Catherine Millot writes that Genet wanted 'to carry out triumphal reversals and heroic overthrowings, taking his inspiration from the message of the Gospels: the first shall be last and the last shall be first. The wretched of the earth are the elect of the poet and his gaze becomes one with God's as he looks upon us.' Genet therefore accords a redemptive value to perdition.[47] This, let me add, is not a feature which is specific to him; like Bataille, like Pierre Rivière and so many others, Genet merely puts his faith in the old Western elaboration of a fantasy of omnipotence which simultaneously entails a devaluing of what is relative and an identification of the absolute as nothing with the absolute as everything.

In this last chapter, I have tried to show how modern ideas of emancipation are underlaid by a confrontational stance linked to an old scenario of heroism and a conception of the world founded upon two levels of reality. We must remember that in the Western tradition there is no ideal which does not entail some form of transcendence of the human condition, and does not aim for a 'solution'. Wisdom, kindness and tact are easy to deal with, but they lack a dramatic side. So – no Chinese-style sages, but saints, Prometheuses and the deranged.

Conclusion

So long as we imagine that malice is attributable only to external causes, all manner of hopes are allowed: a renewed and harmonious society, the new man, brotherhood, the end of exploitation, the eradication of racism, and so on. If, instead, we admit that the inner root of malice cannot be torn out, it means recognizing that there is no solution.

But recognizing that there is no solution does not mean that there is nothing we can do. What can we do to improve ourselves and to improve society? The preceding pages obviously do not supply the answers; all the same, they make it possible to outline some suggestions.

Let us take first of all the question of personal improvement. Moral self-enhancement is not in fashion; these days, private life and close relationships are psychologized; it is relationships at a distance that are moralized. These are the province of what I have called the 'triangle of moral relations' (the denunciation of evil, compassion for victims) whose domain is political, social and humanitarian. Even if it is better to understand than to condemn, this apportioning is questionable. The fact that understanding is called for does not in fact mean that the issue of the good and the harm we do is no longer to be addressed. To be concerned about getting on well or getting on better is a legitimate, even commendable, preoccupation; this preoccupation leads us to address the issue of becoming better differently, but it does not make it go away.

The issue of 'the puritanism of good feeling' has come up a number of times in this book. In it I saw a form of auto-idealization. This is based upon the following line of reasoning: I can clearly distinguish good from evil; when I see a persecutor and his victim, I align myself with the good; therefore, I am good. This complacent sophism obviously runs counter to self-improvement, since the assumption is that perfection has already been acquired.

Self-improvement, therefore, involves a process of de-idealization. It is a matter of recognizing the ambivalence of our fount of limitlessness – in other words, recognizing that the forces of life and the forces which impel us to malice feed upon the same source within us. These forces, therefore, are neither good nor evil in themselves; everything depends upon the relations they form or do not form with the other extreme: limitation.

Let us take an example. We can experience a feeling without thereby realizing that we feel it, or we can know that we feel it but be mistaken about its nature: we can not stand a particular person for this or that reason, and this precise opinion relieves us from an accurate perception of the feelings we experience about him or her, or presents these feelings as being justified (he is the aggressor; we are the victim). In this altogether banal instance, the forces which direct our behaviour with regard to the person in question avoid the limitation which, were it to be applied to these forces, would modify them. Such a limitation might be the mental act of identifying the feeling experienced, and recognizing it as being unjustified. 'Having a mind filled with hatred,' says an old Buddhist text, 'the monk knows: "this is a mind filled with hatred"; whenever malice is in him, he knows: "malice is in me".'[1] The way in which the process of delimitation operates is paradoxical: I discover myself in the act of harbouring bad feelings – of hatred, of envy, a wish to supplant the other, to make him disappear; so there I am, less good and less justified than I wanted to believe; the boundary between good and bad no longer runs outside me, it runs within me; I have de-idealized myself (a little). In recompense for this loss, however, my bad feelings have become less intractable than they were when

I misrecognized them; they have entered an area of differentiation which, by putting them in touch with other aspects of what I am and what reality is, opens them up to a degree of elaboration, and directs them towards a relative viability.

It is inevitable that we should experience bad feelings, and this is why they pose problems for us which are comparable to the problem posed for puritanism by sexual desire. Recognizing one's own bad feelings (that is to say, simultaneously identifying them and acknowledging that they come from within us and do not just come down to a justified reaction) is costly; but not recognizing them is equally costly. Recognizing them means simultaneously losing the self-idealization to which we attached our sense of worth, and losing the wholeness from which we derived a narcissistic satisfaction. Not recognizing them means limiting one's life to the circle of good feeling; it means abandoning energy and relinquishing it to a poisoned and poisonous fate. There is therefore some advantage in taming one's own malice, which in part compensates for the loss this recognition entails. In this sense, reading this book may have given the reader some relief – a relief which, in the end, is not very different from the kind supplied by action films: the pleasure of connecting with a part of one's self which is full of life, a part which the puritanism of good feeling forces one to go without.

Let us leave the question of self-improvement, and move on to the general issue of improving society. On this point, what the preceding pages essentially suggest is that we should mistrust the way in which morality is inclined to portray malice: as something which the discourse of good should be able to act upon. More than once I have stressed the fact that, in order to understand malice, we must distinguish between the *subject of existence* and the *subject of knowledge*. In fact, as soon as we profess moral *ideas*, we are led to believe that the subject of knowledge has the power to overshadow and govern the subject of existence. It is pleasant for us to imagine that we are the masters of our actions, especially when they correspond to the ideas we profess. As a result, we overvalue the importance of the existential fabric which supports our way of being and behaving. By 'existential fabric' I mean all the density of life in society in which we are enmeshed, with its different kinds of relations (familial, friendship, professional) and its different layers of constraints and possibilities (the space of the city, the way in which time is used, relations between the past and the future, economic life, juridical and political institutions, etc.). Admittedly, there are cases where only the principles to which we make reference command our actions; but these are precisely the cases in which we are not engaged in a relationship with the other; in order that morality, law or regulation can have the only say, there must be some disaffiliation, or the relationship must be a relationship at a distance (having to do only with the idea we form of others).

Being decent, just and benevolent is a way of existing. Being malicious is equally a way of existing. It is therefore essential to distinguish between morality as something that offers us a goal and morality as a discourse which sees itself as a means of action. We can acknowledge an absolute value in good, and this does not alter the fact that the discourse which proclaims and points out this absolute value will itself only ever have a relative power. Aiming to transform people through preaching means believing that it is possible to raise oneself up from the ground by pulling oneself up by one's own bootstraps. To grasp a situation solely in moral terms is therefore ultimately immoral; it implies a certain laziness, a refusal of the effort which is necessary in order to discern in the situation those specific features which one nevertheless needs to know and understand in order to act better. This means, for example, perhaps doubting the potential efficacy of lessons in civic and moral education in secondary schools, a measure which is envisaged whenever people are faced with 'the violence of those young people who lack guidance'. In fact, if words do have the power to offer guidance, it is only if they are articulated as lived experience. Consequently, civic education should not be separated from the practice of relationships within the school, first and foremost those irksome everyday questions of discipline. However noble they may be, ideas in themselves alone do not change our ways of being. In order to do this, these ideas have to be translated a little less into discourse and a little more into the real conditions which determine the forms of coexistence. Morality can regulate relationships, but it cannot constitute them (in this sense, there are no moral relationships). The moral will to improvement must therefore take into account the constitution of human relationships, and take a close interest in the complexity of the factors which determine them.

These observations are meant to draw the reader's attention to the limitations of this study. It will, I hope, be of help in recognizing the inner spring of malice, and understanding better the discernible effects that flow from it; but, as I pointed out in the Introduction, this is not enough for us to grasp everything in manifestations of malice which is attributable to a specific historical and social context. I would therefore like to finish by offering some pointers whose intention is to link the issue of the *inner* spring of malice to the other issue of *external* social conditions in which malice comes about. For the sake of convenience, I shall present them by dividing the span of human relationships into three main groups:

1. the set of relationships within which individuals mutually produce a sense of their existence. This set will be discussed in terms of coexistence, being 'in a group', or affiliation;
2. the set of relationships within which if the existence of one is to grow, the existence of the other must diminish. Here there is antagonism, malice and destruction;
3. the set of instances in which the other is external to our sphere of existence: distancing, avoidance, neutralization.

In a number of cases we can observe an intersection or an oscillation between the first two sets[2] – either by individuals or by groups which exist on the basis of something they have in common: an attachment to the same activity, the same places, the same things or the same values. All of them desire whatever they see as sustaining their existence. This attachment compels them to an understanding of their common interest, that of preserving material resources, institutions and practices which enable each of them to associate their well-being with that of the others. But this attachment drives them equally in another direction: the desire to have more than the other or to have what the other has; the desire to have a better place than the other or to take the other's place. At the same time as they maintain their affiliations, material and non-material possessions fuel their rivalries. The fact that no society can ever achieve harmony only renders more precious and more interesting the multiple arrangements and dispositions which preserve, to some degree or other, a kind of balance, or enable this balance to be improved.

Here is an example of ordinary malice prompted by an attachment to the same things. The ground floor of a house goes up for sale. A couple move in with their two children, a boy and a girl, who are now teenagers. An old lady has been living for years on the first floor. The small garden at the back of the house is tied to the ground-floor property, and from now on the lady must stay within her legal territory. From her window she watches these young people entertaining friends and sunbathing on the lawn; envy intensifies her disapproval. She has to put up with the noise of their voices and their music; she complains, she calls the police. She is elderly and alone; this is all she has left: filling the emptiness of her days with worrying about the neighbours, feeling that, whatever their own priorities, she is determined to occupy a place in their minds regardless. She no longer has any other way of being, so she cannot help herself, she will invade them by means of legal proceedings, she will sacrifice her savings to this end. A social worker who assumes the role of mediator tries hard to calm the situation down; he approaches it with patience; he is used to conflict between neighbours: the adjacent other, the other who defiles me, the persecutor whom I dream of doing away with.

The reversal of the friend into foe, confrontations and duels – all this exerts a certain fascination. As a result, whenever we tend towards violence, we often neglect the third set (distancing, neutralization), which, by its very nature, tends to go unnoticed. None the less it plays a significant role, both in the most peaceable varieties of social life and in the processes which bring about malice. Each one of us distinguishes between those with whom we have a bond and others. Within the circle of our intimates, there are times when we are in touch and times when contact is suspended (it is in fact intolerable to be compelled to maintain active contact all the time, even with people we love). This alternation is already observable in the infant, along with the neutralization of people who are unfamiliar to him or her. We can quite easily include everyone in the sphere of our knowledge (for example, when we read a newspaper), but in our sphere of existence we can include only a limited number of people, and even this involves alternating activation and deactivation. The process of neutralization – this point must be emphasized – is therefore, in itself, both healthy and universal. Moreover, it is inscribed within language in the form of the third person: all the *they* are neutralized by a conversation in which *I* and *you* take part.

Nevertheless, neutralization is just as subject to instability as coexistence. Coexistence can turn into rivalry; neutralization can easily turn into disparagement and hostility. How does this shift take place? The *they* and the *them* do not disappear from my field of consciousness, I know that they exist, I often even see them, I run into them in the street. But I can exist just as well without them, between us there is not that shared existence which comes about through attachment to the same thing, participation in the same sphere of life. The *they* and the *them* exist in other spheres: what matters to them is not what matters to me. And this is where their existence can begin to annoy me. What is important to them indirectly reduces the scope of what is important to me; they have no loyalty to what upholds my idea of my own worth; they live as if what is important to me (to us) did not exist. Thus, indirectly, they belittle that through which I value myself. Our differences impoverish us (they enrich us only if, in the first place, we have found *common ground*). If, moreover, I have to rub shoulders with these others while they do not practise the customs and manners which, in my circle, constitute an *area of concordance*, enabling me to know where I am with my interlocutor or my partner, then I am suddenly in a situation where it is impossible to place boundaries and to locate what they want from me. I do not know how to manage a relationship with them. I feel powerless; they frighten me. It is as if I were being confronted by some unbounded presence, so that I cannot stop myself from projecting upon them the fantasy of absolute evil. All these others therefore expose me to the humiliation and threat of feeling myself sinking into the loathesome morass of disparate humanity. Thus, as the members of *us* mutually contribute to the maintenance and reinforcement of their sense of existing, they are led also to draw an extra quantity of existence from the *them*, which is precisely what they get from being malicious towards them. As I have shown in the course of the preceding chapters, disparagement and hatred, destruction and the inflicting of suffering, *primo*, bring the *us* a more-being which benevolence would be unable to provide; *secundo*, it supplies reparation for the less-being inflicted by any non-allegiance towards the attributes to which are attached a sense of worth; *tertio*, they make it possible to enjoy a wholeness which is the mirror-image of the bad limitlessness projected on to these others.

The sequence I have just outlined leads me to dispute the thesis maintained by Pierre Clastres in *Archéologie de la violence. La guerre dans les sociétés primitives.*[3] Clastres's thesis presupposes a conception of human beings from which the idea of an inner spring of malice is absent. For him, the permanent state of war carried out by numerous primitive societies responds to a function – not the group function of bringing about the triumph of its own interests (economic stakes are either absent or reduced to pretexts), but the function of keeping groups separate, and thus preventing the formation of a state: so the goal of war is fragmentation. To support this thesis, Clastres (like Carl Schmitt, but for a different reason) has to allow that 'Others are categorized from the outset as friends and foes'. Clastres therefore pays no attention to the – albeit widely practised – option of categorizing others within a neutral zone. As a result, he loses sight of one aspect of violence which is, however, fundamental: the shift from neutrality to hostility. The avoidance of other groups would be enough to preserve each individual group from the formation of a state. If hostility and war are added to this distancing, there are therefore other reasons involved – rather as in the banal case of car drivers who take advantage of the protective distance afforded by the glass-screened capsule of their vehicles in order to take out their resentments on pedestrians or other drivers.

Here are two examples in which we can see how the shift from neutrality to aggressive disaffiliation takes place.

The first example. A number of pupils from the same class are accustomed to playing together during recreation. Those they do not play with are therefore, in their view, to some degree or other, neutral. Among those who are 'neutralized', there are some children whose social background means that they have very different ways of being from theirs. When it comes to these children, for the reasons I have given above, the neutralization is therefore tinged with a degree of hostility. This, however, remains contained, for the simple reason that because these children have bonded together, they make themselves feared. On the other hand, one of the pupils in the class who is also an outsider to the group which plays together (he is not their type) seems, moreover, to be isolated. The members of the little group can therefore gang up against him. They make him the butt of their sarcasm. One day, excited by the pleasure they effortlessly obtain through this, and emboldened by their impunity, they attack him ferociously. The next day, the victim is absent. The child is depressed and ill, unwilling to return to school. His parents complain to the teacher.

The second example. In July 1942, the 101st Battalion of German police reservists was sent to Josefow, in Poland. It was essentially made up of workmen and clerks from the city of Hamburg. The head of the battalion explained to them that they had to round up the one thousand eight hundred Jews living there, and slaughter the women, children and old men in the nearby forest. For men who knew nothing of the executioner's trade, this day of killings was very testing. Some of them shied away from their task; the only punishment in store for them was to be regarded by their comrades as people who would let you down, or to be considered as not 'real men'. There were others who found among the Jews of Josefow someone or other they had known in Hamburg. In the evening, everyone got drunk. Other operations were to follow; gradually they came to take them in their stride. New techniques of killing, combined with anti-Semitic propaganda, helped them to forge a gap between themselves and their victims.[4]

I told this story (as well as the one about soldiers in Vietnam who were unable to stop themselves from vomiting the first time they were ordered to machine-gun civilians from their helicopters) to a friend with a responsible job in a large company. He told me that he himself had been given the task of sacking a number of people. He knew them slightly; he had even chatted with some of them in the cafeteria. He told me that with the first person he had felt very uncomfortable, and had no idea how to deal with it. The most difficult part of all was to go against a relationship which, although it was not close, was nonetheless part of the fact of working in the same company, and therefore of an affiliation. Little by little, he had managed to steel himself, he had learned to detach himself from his interlocutors and to say what had to be said. And then he had observed that, thanks to the stance of disaffiliation which he had been able to establish, beyond the displeasure which persisted there was something else that intervened. Something which, now that he came to talk about it to me, he identified as a kind of satisfaction: through the role which he fulfilled, it was the voice of necessity that spoke; a reality greater than him communicated its force to him, and he was participating in this sovereign power.

Every form of relationship between human beings, even if it contains something intolerable, engenders an 'addiction'. For just as water, with its tendency to flow, embraces the contours of the ground, the necessity to exist which drives us receives the imprint of the conjuncture of relations in which we find ourselves. Water (the necessity to exist) can be encouraged by the slope offered by its situation; in this case learning to exist in this situation is easy and immediately profitable (the children of whom I spoke in my first example). The water can instead be held back by obstacles (this was the case for the German policemen in Poland). However, as soon as the situation offers a gap between the 'affiliated' and the 'neutralized', or between strong and weak affiliations, the necessity to exist turns this breach to its advantage. Striving blindly to find a foothold, it bases its sphere of existence upon the affiliations which are imposed upon it, and, in contrast, avoids those which would break its unity or reduce its scope.

Notes

Introduction

1. Primo Levi, *Le devoir de mémoire*, interview with A. Bravo and F. Cereja, Mille et une nuits, Paris 1995, pp. 40–41.

2. *In Wickedness* (Routledge Classics, London and New York, first published 1984), Mary Midgley raised the very question I attempt to answer in this book. 'There is a real difficulty', she says, 'in understanding how people, including ourselves, can act as badly as they sometimes do.' It is therefore a matter of understanding 'what goes on in the heart of the wicked' (pp. 9, 4). Midgley argues, as I do, against the tendency to believe that malice is not rooted within human nature, and is the result of purely external circumstances. She ends her book with a discussion of Freud's theory of the death instinct. My book begins where hers ends: the pages that follow could be read as an effort to acquaint the reader with the psychological and clinical facts which underlie the theory of the death instinct. As set out by Freud, this theory is somewhat unconvincing; if, on the other hand, we have some knowledge of the physical facts which caused him to believe that there is such a thing as a death instinct (writers like John Milton and Mary Shelley, who have plumbed the depths of the will to destroy, are immensely helpful here), we can, I believe, attain a better understanding of 'what goes on in the heart of the wicked'.

3. See, for example, François Furet, *Le passé d'une illusion. Essai sur l' idée communiste au XXᵉ siècle*, Robert Laffont/Calman-Lévy, Paris 1995.

4. John Locke, *Some Thoughts Concerning Education*, ed. John W. and Jean S. Yolton, Clarendon Press, Oxford 1989, pp. 163–4.

5. Jean-Jacques Rousseau, *Émile or On Education*, trans. Allan Bloom, Penguin, Harmondsworth 1991, p. 92.

6. Longinus, 'On the Sublime', Chapter XXV, in *Aristotle, The Poetics, Longinus on the Sublime, Demetrius on Style*, trans. W. Hamilton Fyfe, Heinemann, London 1928.
7. I can agree with Konrad Lorenz on this point; see *On Aggression*, trans. Marjorie Latzke, Routledge, London 1996.
8. See Immanual Kant, *Religion within the Limits of Reason Alone*, Book 1, trans. with Introduction by Theodore M. Green and Hoyt H. Hudson, Harper & Brothers, New York 1960, especially Chapter 3, 'Man Is Bad by Nature'.
9. I have made a much more detailed examination of the issue of analysing and interpreting narratives in my account of storytelling in the European oral tradition (*La pensée des contes*, Anthropos, Paris 2001).
10. This preparation is to some small extent illustrated by my study on domestic quarrels (*La scène de ménage*, Denoël, Paris 1987), and in a short story written in homage to Ingmar Bergman ('Duels', *Le cinéma des écrivains*, Cahiers du cinéma, Paris 1995).
11. Norman Cohn, *Cosmos, Chaos and the World to Come: The Ancient Roots of Apocalyptic Faith*, Yale, Newhaven, CT/London 1993.
12. Tzvetan Todorov, *Mémoire du mal, tentation du bien. Enquête sur le siècle*, Robert Laffont, Paris 2000, p. 214.
13. Alain Finkielkraut, *Une voix qui vient de l' autre rive*, Gallimard, Paris 2000, pp. 71, 75, 77.
14. Todorov, *Mémoire du mal*, p. 154.

1 The Price of Monotheism

1. In the Book of Job, Satan is not yet the Devil; he is an angel, a counsellor and an emissary from Yahweh. See Norman Cohn, *Cosmos, Chaos and the World to Come*, Yale, Newhaven, CT/London 1993, ch. 10, III.
2. Here I am thinking of Jean Bottéro's article 'Le problème du mal', in the *Dictionnaire des mythologies*, ed. Yves Bonnefoy, Flammarion, Paris 1981, vol. II, p. 56–64.
3. Primo Levi, *If This Is a Man*, in *If This Is a Man, The Truce*, trans. Stuart Woolf, Vintage, New York 1996, p. 35.
4. Ferdinando Camon, *Conversations avec Primo Levi*, Gallimard, Paris 1991. See also Myriam Anissimov, *Primo Levi ou la tragédie d' un optimiste*, Lattès, Paris 1996.
5. See F.Jullien, *Procès ou création*, Seuil, Paris 1989, ch. 5, 'Ni Créateur ni création'; J.Gernet, *Chine et Christianisme*, Gallimard, Paris 1982, part V, 'Ciel des Chinois, Dieu des Chrétiens'.
6. Haris Jonas, *Le concept de Dieu après Auschwitz*, Payot-Rivages, Paris 1994.
7. Galen, *De usu partium*, XI, 14, quoted by J. Pigeaud in his discussion of Longinus, *On the Sublime*, Rivages, Paris 1993, p. 22.

8. Exodus 19: 16–19;20: 18–19; 24: 17 (Authorized King James Version of the Bible with Apocrypha, ed. Robert Carroll and Stephen Pickett, Oxford World's Classics, Oxford 1997).

9. See Jean Bottéro, *Naissance de Dieu, la Bible et l'historien*, Folio, Gallimard, Paris 1996, p. 59.

10. On Yahweh's superiority to Baal, see I Kings, 18: 19–40.

11. Michael Walzer, *Interpretation and Social Criticism*, Harvard University Press, Cambridge, MA/London 1987, pp. 89–93.

12. See Bottéro, *Naissance de Dieu*, pp. 96–7, p. 160.

13. Ibid., 'Les origines de l'univers selon la Bible', 'Les cosmogonies sous-jacentes', pp. 243 ff. See also S.G.F. Brandon, *Creation Legends of the Ancient Near East*, Hodder & Stoughton, London 1963, pp. 119 ff.

14. Psalm LXXIV: 12–17.

15. Marc Augé, *Génie du paganisme*, Gallimard, Paris 1982, p. 104.

16. Parmenides, fragments 8, 6–21, in *Plato and Parmenides*, trans with running commentary by Francis Macdonald Cornford, Kegan Paul, London 1939, p. 36.

17. The Book of Job 40: 15–19; 41: 1, 9–11, 33.

18. See Bothéro, *Naissance de Dieu*, esp. pp. 108–109, 178–9.

19. In *La pensée des contes*, Anthropos, Paris 2001, 'Postface sur le symbolisme', I make an effort to show why, instead of attempting to formulate the meaning of a narrative (assuming that there is one), one should above all inquire into the source of the interest the narrative arouses in its audience.

20. See J.Richer's article 'Révolte. Mythes romantiques du révolté et de la victime', in *Dictionnaire des mythologies*, Flammarion, Paris 1981, vol. II, pp. 324–8.

21. Edmund Burke, *A Philosophical Enquiry into the Origin of Our Ideas of the Sublime and Beautiful*, ed. James T. Boulton, Basil Blackwell, Oxford 1987, p. 64.

22. In *Le complexe de Léonard* (colloquium), *Le Nouvel Observateur*, Lattès, Paris 1984, pp. 335–7.

23. Quoted by Anissimov, *Primo Levi ou la tragédie d' un optimiste*, p. 559.

24. Primo Levi's reflections on Job are taken from *La ricerca delle radici. Antologia personale*, Einaudi, Turin 1981, p. 5 and *passim*.

25. Levi, *If This Is a Man*, pp. 395–6.

26. Alain Badiou, *L' éthique. Essai sur la conscience du mal*, Hatier, Paris 1994, p. 55. (Published in translation as *Ethics: An Essay on the Understanding of Evil*, Verso, London and New York 2001).

2   The Spectre of Absolute Evil

1. I am drawing on the papers from the international conference on *La notion de personne en Afrique noire*, organized by G. Dieterlen, Éditions du CNRS,

Paris 1973; and on Charles-Henri Pradelles de Latour's excellent study, *Le crâne qui parle. Ethnopsychanalyse en pays Bamiléké*, EPEL, Paris 1996.

2. I would therefore not say, as Melanie Klein does in her *Psychoanalysis of Children*, that such powers of annihilation actually stand for the parents.

3. Georges Bataille, 'L'homme souverain de Sade', *L'érotisme*, 10/18, 1965, p. 185.

4. Quoted by Cathy Bernheim, *Mary Shelley, qui êtes-vous?*, La Manufacture, Lyons 1988, p. 90.

5. See, for example, A. de Baecque, *La gloire et l' effroi. Sept morts sous la terreur*, Grasset, Paris 1997, chapter on Madame Necker.

6. See M. Summers, *The Gothic Quest: A History of the Gothic Novel*, Russell & Russell, New York 1964, pp. 121–2, 291.

7. Mary Shelley said this in the preface to a later edition of *Frankenstein* published in 1831.

8. 'A Passional Karma', in *In Ghostly Japan*, Charles E.Tuttle & Co., Rutland, VT/Tokyo 1971.

9. Quoted by Michael Paul Rogin in *Fathers and Children: Andrew Jackson and the Subjugation of the American Indian*, Knopf, New York 1975, p. 120.

10. Ibid., p. 123.

11. See D.W. Winnicott's *Playing and Reality*; also O. Mannoni's very enlightening suggestions on the disidentification which enables conscious imitation ('La désidentification', in *Le Moi et l'Autre*, introduced by Maud Mannoni, Denoël, Paris 1985).

3   Victor Frankenstein's Excess

1. All quotations from *Frankenstein* are from the Penguin edition with introduction and notes by Maurice Hindle, Harmondsworth 1985 [trans.].

2. See Christopher Small, *Mary Shelley's Frankenstein: Tracing the Myth*, University of Pittsburgh Press, Pittsburgh, PA 1973, p. 107 (first published 1972 as *Ariel Like a Harpy: Shelley, Mary and Frankenstein*).

3. *The Letters of Percy Bysshe Shelley*, ed Frederick L. Jones, Clarendon Press, Oxford 1964, vol. II, p. 211.

4. Quoted by Philippe Lacoue-Labarthe, *La fiction du politique (Heidegger, l'art et la politique)*, Association des Publications près les Universités de Strasbourg, Strasbourg 1987, p. 53.

5. Quoted by D. Colas, in *Le léninisme*, PUF, Paris 1982, pp. 267–8. See also ch. 4, 'Les modèles: l'orchestre, l'armée, la machine, l'usine'.

4   The Infernal Couple

1. For this chapter I draw on my earlier research study, *La scène de ménage*, Denoël, Paris 1987.
2. John Milton, *Paradise Lost*, Book X, lines 743–5 (in John Milton, *The Complete English Poems*, ed. Gordon Campbell, Everyman's Library, London 1992).
3. See Phyllis Grosskurth, *Byron: The Flawed Angel*, Hodder & Stoughton, London 1997.
4. Milton, *Paradise Lost*, Book X, lines 728–37. These lines appear very close to the ones Mary chose as the epigraph to her novel.
5. Quoted by Christopher Small, *Mary Shelley's Frankenstein: Tracing the Myth*, University of Pittsburgh Press, Pittsburgh, PA 1973, p. 21.
6. Maurice Leenhardt, *Do kamo. La personne et le mythe dans le monde mélanésien*, Tel, Gallimard, Paris 1985, pp. 88–94.
7. Fyodor Dostoevsky, *Memoirs from the House of the Dead*, trans Jessie Coulson, Oxford University Press, Oxford 1983, Part Two, ch. 4.

5   Pity for the Monster

1. It is very evident in, for example, Adam Smith's *Theory of Moral Sentiments*. See Luc Boltanski, *La souffrance à distance. Morale humanitaire, médias et politique*, Métailié, Paris 1993.
2. Edmund Burke, *A Philosophical Enquiry into the Origin of Our Ideas of the Sublime and Beautiful*, ed. James T. Boulton, Basil Blackwell, Oxford 1987, pp. 44–5.
3. John Milton, *Paradise Lost*, Book II, lines 666–73.
4. Burke, *The Sublime and Beautiful*, pp. 50–51.
5. Longinus, 'On the Sublime', in *Aristotle, The Poetics, Longinus on the Sublime, Demetrius on Style*, trans. W. Hamilton Fyfe, Heinemann, London 1928, ch. VII, 2, p. 139.
6. We find an apt reference in Boileau to Corneille's famous lines: 'What would you he had done against three men? – Met his death'; and Diderot, too, quoted them as a classic example of the sublime (Boileau, preface to Longinus' treatise *On the Sublime*, in *Œuvres complètes*, La Pléiade, Gallimard, Paris 1966, p. 340; Diderot, *Traité du beau*, in *Œuvres*, La Pléiade, Gallimard, Paris 1992, p. 1099.
7. In the *Critique of the Faculty of Judgement* (1790), and starting with *The Sublime and Beautiful* (1764). See B. Saint Girons, *Fiat Lux. Une philosophie du sublime*, Quai Voltaire, Paris 1993.
8. Burke, *The Sublime and Beautiful*, pp. 87–9.

9. *Le Figaro*, 17 October 1883. Quoted by Jacques Borgé and Nicolas Viasnoff, *Archives de l'Indochine*, Michèle Trinckvel, Paris 1995.

10. Lynn Hunt *The Family Romance of the French Revolution*, University of California Press, Berkeley, CA/Routledge, London 1992.

11. See J.S. Spink, 'Les avatars du sentiment de l'existence de Locke à Rousseau', *Dix-huitième siècle*, no. 10, 1978, pp. 269–98, where he quotes the passage from Buffon (vol. 1 of *Histoire naturelle*, 1749).

12. John Locke, *Essay Concerning Human Understanding*, ed. John W. Yolton, Everyman's University Library, Dent, London 1976, Bk two, ch. 1. This is the view of Jean-Jacques Lecercle, *Frankenstein: mythe et philosophie*, PUF, Paris 1988, p. 34.

13. Milton, *Paradise Lost*, Book IV, lines 449–52; Book VIII, lines 261–3.

14. Ibid., Book VIII, lines 250–51.

15. A play which Mary Shelley might have known in the English translation which appeared in 1792 (see M. Summers, *The Gothic Quest: A History of the Gothic Novel*, Russell & Russell, New York 1964).

16. H.P. Lovecraft, *The Outsider, and others . . .* collected by August Derleth and Donald Wandrai, Arkham House, Sauk City, WI 1939.

6 Thought and Reason versus Literature and Passion

1. Abbé Raynal, *Histoire philosophique et politique des établissements et du commerce des Européens dans les deux Indes*, vol. 7, pp. 138–9, 160–61. Quoted by Michèle Duchet, *Anthropologie et histoire au siècle des Lumières*, Albin Michel, Paris 1995, p. 216.

2. Letter of November 1760, in Denis Diderot, *Correspondance*, Minuit, Paris 1957, vol. 3, p. 226.

3. Louis Antoine Léon de Saint-Just, *Discours sur la Constitution de la France*, speech made to the National Convention on 24 April 1793, Mille et une nuits, Paris 1996, p. 9.

4. Letter of December 1769, in Diderot, *Correspondance*, vol. 9, p. 236.

5. C.F. Volney, *La loi naturelle* and *Leçons d' histoire*, introduced by J. Gaulmier, Garnier, Paris 1980, p. 46.

6. On this point see, for example, A.O. Hirschman, *The Passions and the Interests: Political Arguments for Capitalism before its Triumph*, Princeton University Press, Princeton, NJ 1977; P. Tillich, *La naissance de l'esprit moderne et la theologie protestante*, Éditions du Cerf, Paris 1972.

7. William Godwin, *Enquiry Concerning Political Justice and its Influence on Morals and Happiness*, 4th edn, J. Watson, London 1842, vol. 1, p. 3. See also p. 19, where Godwin pictures 'an education precisely equal and eminently wise', producing what can be seen as a type of Émile.

8. Benjamin Constant, *De la justice politique*, Presses de l' Université de Laval, Quebec 1972, p. 372.
9. See Christopher Small, *Mary Shelley's Frankenstein: Tracing the Myth*, University of Pittsburgh Press, Pittsburgh, PA 1973, p. 23.
10. All quotations from *Caleb Williams* are taken from the Penguin edition, ed. Maurice Hindle, Harmondsworth 1988 [Trans.].
11. Jean-Jacques Rousseau, *Reveries of the Solitary Walker*, trans. Peter France, Penguin, Harmondsworth 1979, p. 90.
12. See Anne K. Mellor, *Mary Shelley: Her Life, Her Fiction, Her Monsters*, Routledge, New York 1988, pp. 70–88, 237–8. See also Lisa Catron and Edgar Newman, 'Frankenstein: les Lumières et la Révolution comme monstre', *Annales historiques de la Révolution française*, no. 2, 1993, esp. pp. 208–11.
13. Monette Vacquin, *Frankenstein ou les délires de la raison*, François Bourin, Paris 1989, p. 219. See also Dominique Lecourt, *Prométhée, Faust, Frankenstein*, Les empêcheurs de penser en rond, Paris 1996.
14. I refer here in particular to Christopher Small's conclusion (*Mary Shelley's Frankenstein*, op cit). I hasten to add that this work is far superior to its own conclusion, and that I benefited a great deal from reading it.
15. Godwin *Enquiry Concerning Political Justice*, vol. 2, p. 27.
16. See J. Delumeau's article, 'La pastorale de la peur chez les Puritains', in A. Morvan, ed, *La peur, actes du colloque organisé par le Centre de Recherches sur l'Angleterre des Tudors à la Régence*, University of Lille, Lille 1985, pp. 14, 20.
17. Ibid., p. 16.
18. I am thinking particularly about the novels and short stories written by Jean-Pierre Camus, a disciple of Saint Francis de Sales. See Sylvie de Baecque, *Le salut par l'excès. La poétique d' un évêque romancier, Jean-Pierre Camus, 1608–1662*, Champion, Paris 1999.
19. Milton, *Paradise Lost*, Book VIII, lines 415–29.
20. Thomas Moore, *Life of Lord Byron with his Letters and Journals*, John Murray, London 1851, vol. 5, p. 305.

7   Good Feeling

1. William Godwin, *Enquiry Concerning Political Justice and its Influence on Morals and Happiness*, 4th edn. J. Watson, London 1842, vol. 1, pp. 66–8.
2. Jean-Jacques Rousseau, *Reveries of the Solitary Walker*, trans. Peter France, Penguin, Harmondsworth 1979, pp. 27–8.
3. Ibid., p. 31.
4. Jean-Jacques Rousseau, *Confessions*, ed. and introduced by P.N. Furbank, Everyman's Library, London 1992, vol. 2, p. 71.
5. Ibid., p. 97.

6. Ibid., vol. 2, p. 74; vol. 1, p. 304.
7. Ibid., vol. 2, p. 74.
8. Rousseau, *Reveries of the Solitary Walker*, p. 52.
9. See in particular ch. 8, Book 1, of Jean-Jacques Rousseau, *The Social Contract*, which celebrates the passage from the state of nature to the social state.
10. See Luc Boltanski's study of media compassion, *La souffrance à distance. Morale humanitaire, médias et politique*, Métailié, Paris 1993.
11. See Charles Taylor, *Sources of the Self: The Making of the Modern Identity*, Cambridge University Press, Cambridge 1989, p. 261.
12. Friedrich Schlegel, *Discours sur la mythologie*, quoted by Philippe Lacoue-Labarthe and Jean-Louis Nancy, in *L'absolu littéraire*, Seuil, Paris 1978, p. 312. See also J.-M. Schaeffer, *La naissance de la littérature. La théorie esthétique du roman-tisme allemand*, Presses de l'École Normale Supérieure, Paris 1983.

8   Idyllic Completeness, Violent Completeness

1. John Milton, *Paradise Lost*, Book IV, lines 362–3, 502–11; Book IX, lines 453, 477–9.
2. Augustine, *Confessions*, trans. Maria Boulding, Hodder & Stoughton, London 1997, pp. 46, 44.
3. Milton, *Paradise Lost*, Book II, lines 46–9.
4. René Girard, *Mensonge romantique et vérité romanesque*, Le Livre de Poche, Paris 1982, p. 307.
5. Milton, *Paradise Lost*, Book II, lines 891–7; Book VII, lines 211–15.
6. Ibid., Book III, lines 11–12. See A. Koyré, *Du monde clos à l'univers infini*, Idées, Gallimard, Paris 1973.
7. Ibid., Book II, line 149; Book III, lines 708–11; Book V, lines 577–9.
8. See Giorgio Agamben, *Infancy and History: Essays on the Destruction of Experience*, trans Liz Heron, Verso, London and New York 1993, pp. 22–3.
9. See Giulia Sissa, *Le plaisir et le mal. Philosophie de la drogue*, Odile Jacob, Paris 1977.
10. See Friedrich Nietzsche, *On the Genealogy of Morals*, trans. Douglas Smith, Oxford University Press, Oxford 1996, esp. the first dissertation, [§] 10, 11 and 16.
11. Vincent Descombes, *Le même et l'autre. Quarante-cinq ans de philosophie française (1933–1978)*, Minuit, Paris 1979, p. 193.
12. Regarding the aim of relevance that underlies all speech, I take the liberty of referring to my own book, *La parole intermédiaire*, Seuil, Paris 1978, 'L'énonciation comme rapport à la complétude', pp. 101–12.
13. See J. Soustelle, *La pensée cosmologique des anciens Mexicains*, Hermann, Paris 1940; Christophe Duverger, *La fleur létale. Économie du sacrifice aztèque*, Seuil, Paris 1979.

14. Duverger, *La fleur létale*, pp. 50–51; emphasis added.

15. Ibid., pp. 217–24.

16. Here I draw on Martine Van Woerkens's detailed study *Le voyageur étranglé. L'Inde des Thugs, le colonialisme et l'imaginaire*, Albin Michel, Paris 1995.

17. G.E. Lessing, *The Education of the Human Race*, preceded by the Masonic Dialogues, trans. F.W. Robertson, Kegan Paul & Co., London 1896.

18. John Paul II, *Evangelium vitae, An Encyclical on the Value and Inviolability of Human Life*, Veritas Publications, Dublin 1995.

19. Ibid., p. 10.

20. John Paul II is faithful to the earliest tradition.Tertullian (who died at the beginning of the third century) was already teaching that 'all fruit is in the seed', that the soul comes into being with the seed and is not given to the body only at the first breath taken by the newborn, as the Stoics claimed. Tertullian's view also ran counter to Roman law, for which the embryo remained a part of the woman's body. See M. Spanneut, *Le stoïcisme des Pères de l' Église de Clément de Rome à Clément d' Alexandrie*, Seuil, Paris 1957.

21. John Paul II, *Evangelium vitae*, pp. 88–90.

9   The Promethean Revolt

1. See G. McNiece, *Shelley and the Revolutionary Idea*, Harvard University Press, Cambridge, MA 1969, esp. p. 219.

2. Quoted by Christopher Hill, *Milton and the English Revolution*, Faber & Faber, London 1977, p. 206.

3. See Christopher Taylor, *Sources of the Self: The Making of the Modern Identity*, Cambridge University Press, Cambridge 1992, p. 231. See also Locke's treatise on *Civil Government*, 'On Natural Law and Property'.

4. Aeschylus, *Prometheus Bound*, trans Elizabeth Barrett Browning, Players Press, Studio City, CA 1992, p. 19.

5. Ibid., p. 42.

6. Jean Starobinski, *Jean-Jacques Rousseau: la transparence et l'obstacle*, Gallimard, Paris 1987, pp. 286–7.

7. See J.-P. Vernant, *Entre mythe et politique*, Seuil, Paris 1996, for his writings on tragedy, pp. 425–98, esp. p. 437.

8. Nicole Loraux, 'Les damnés de la terre à Troie. Sartre face aux Troyennes d' Euripides', Le Genre humain, no. 29, *Les bons sentiments*, 1995, p. 41.

9. Aeschylus, *Prometheus Bound*, p. 20.

10. Ibid., p. 40.

11. Ibid., pp. 39–42.

12. Ibid., p. 17.

13. Here I draw on R. Trousson, *Le thème de Prométhée dans la littérature européene*,

2 vols, Librairie Droz, Geneva, 2nd edn, 1976. I also wish to thank Yves Hersant for the help he has given me regarding the figure of Prometheus during the Renaissance.

14. See Dominique Lecourt, 'Marx-Prométhée', in *Prométhée, Faust, Frankenstein, Les empêcheurs de penser en rond*, Paris 1996, pp. 60–61.

15. See Paul Bénichou, *Le sacre de l' écrivain, 1750–1830. Essai sur l'avènement d'un pouvoir spirituel laïque dans la France moderne*, José Corti, Paris 1985; *Le temps des prophètes. Doctrines de l' âge romantique*, Gallimard, Paris 1977.

16. See René Koselleck, *Le règne de la critique*, Minuit, Paris 1979.

17. See Norbert Elias, *La civilisation des mœurs*, Calmann-Lévy, Paris 1973; and, also by Norbert Elias, *La société des individus*, Fayard, Paris 1991.

18. It would be a mistake to think that a character can never achieve heroic status in the role of the third party. TzvetanTodorov's *Une tragédie française* (Seuil, Paris 1994) gives an account of a Resistance episode in the Berry region, and provides a good example of a hero as mediator.

19. See Hill, *Milton and the English Revolution*, esp. pp. 92, 180, 428 ff.

20. See Michel Foucault, *'Il faut défendre la société'*, a course of lectures at the Collège de France (1975–1976), Hautes Études, Gallimard, Seuil, Paris 1997.

21. Ibid., pp. 62, 68. See also pp. 44–5.

22. Alexandre Kojève, *Introduction à la lecture de Hegel*, Gallimard, Paris 1992, p. 26 (first edn 1943).

23. Ibid., p. 27.

24. Ibid., p. 33.

25. See Michèle Duchet, *Anthropologie et histoire au siècle des Lumières*, Albin Michel, Paris 1995, p. 140 ff, 'Le thème de la révolte'; and p. 175.

26. Aimé Césaire, *Et les chiens se taisaient*, Présence africaine, Paris/Dakar 1989, p. 68.

27. Frantz Fanon, *Peaux noires, masques blancs*, Points Seuil, Paris 1975, p. 90.

28. Frantz Fanon, *The Wretched of the Earth*, trans Constance Farrington, Penguin, Harmondsworth 1983, p. 36.

29. Ibid.

30. Ibid., p. 28.

31. Ibid., p. 38.

32. Ibid., p. 20.

33. Michael Walzer, *Interpretation and Social Criticism*, Harvard University Press, Cambridge, MA/London 1987.

34. Jean-Paul Sartre, *The Flies and In Camera*, trans. Stuart Gilbert, Hamish Hamilton, London 1946, Act III, pp. 96–7.

35. Julia Kristeva, *Sens et non-sens de la révolte*, Fayard, Paris 1996, p. 336.

36. Herbert Marcuse, *One-dimensional Man*, Routledge & Kegan Paul, London 1964.

37. Simone de Beauvoir, 'Faut-il brûler Sade?', *Les Temps modernes*, January 1952, pp. 1228, 1230; emphasis added.

38. Jean Paulhan, *Œuvres complètes*, Cercle du livre précieux, Paris 1969, vol. 4, pp. 39–40.
39. Jacques Lacan, 'Kant avec Sade', in *Écrits*, Seuil, Paris 1966, pp. 765–6.
40. John Milton, *Paradise Lost*, Book IV, line 110.
41. Paulhan, *Œuvres complètes*, vol. 4, p. 28.
42. *I, Pierre Rivière, having slaughtered my mother, my sister and my brother . . . a case of parricide in the 19th century*, Ed Michel Foucault, Penguin, Harmondsworth 1975 [the quotations that follow are my translations from the original French, *Moi, Pierre Rivière*, Gallimard–Juilliard, Paris 1973 – trans.].
43. *Moi, Pierre Rivière*, pp. 103–4.
44. J.-P. Peter and Jeanne Favret, 'L'animal, le fou, la mort', pp. 254, 251, 250, 252.
45. De Beauvoir, 'Faut-il brûler Sade?', p. 1221.
46. René Étiemble, 'Un mythe explose', *Les Temps modernes*, January 1952, pp. 1264, 1268.
47. Catherine Millot, *Gide Genet Mishima. Intelligence de la perversion*, Gallimard, Paris 1996, pp. 82, 89.

Conclusion

1. Walpola Rahula, *L'enseignement du Bouddha d'après les textes les plus anciens*, Seuil, Paris 1978, pp. 141–2.
2. This is something that is often mentioned by ethnographers – for example, Edward Evans Pritchard in *The Nuer*, Oxford University Press, New York and Oxford 1974.
3. Pierre Clastres, *Archéologie de la violence. La guerre dans les sociétés primitives.* Éditions de l'aube, 1977.
4. See Christopher R. Browning, *Ordinary Men: Reserve Police Battalion 101 and the Final Solution in Poland*, HarperCollins, New York 1992. There are further examples in Françoise Héritier's *De la violence*, Odile Jacob, Paris 1996.

Index

Also by François Flahault

L'extrême existence, Maspéro, 1972.

La Parole intermédiaire, préface de Roland Barthes, Seuil, 1978.

Jeu de Babel. Où le lecteur trouvera matière à inventer des fictions par milliers, Point Hors Ligne, 1984.

La Scène de ménage, Denoël, 1987.

Face à face, histoires de visages, Plon, 1989.

La Pensée des contes, Anthropos, 2001.

Le Sentiment d'exister. Ce soi qui ne va pas de soi, Descartes & Cie, 2002.